The TERMINAL generation

A Revolutionary Revelation

Gary King

The Terminal Generation: A Revolutionary Revelation

ISBN: 978-0-692680-83-4

Gary King
New Life Christian Center
Celina, Ohio
www.NLCC-celina.org

Contents

Foreword

Summary of this book, *The Terminal Generation*

In this book we take a fresh look at the subject of eschatology, which is the study of end-time prophetic events, and are not locked into the traditional thinking and teachings espoused in the last 200 years. The views expressed here are the result of a comparison of what God taught on this subject through the Old Testament prophets with what Jesus taught on this important subject while He was on the earth, and/or what He taught through the apostles from heaven after His ascension.

The basic premise exercised in this comparison is that what Jesus taught in the Old Testament, or what He taught while on the earth, or what He taught after His ascension, would never contradict one another. What Jesus taught on earth was spoken in plain language, whereas other teachings are very parabolic (in heavenly language). In interpreting parabolic language, there can be numerous possibilities as to God's intended meaning. However, many of these possibilities can be eliminated by comparing them with what Jesus taught plainly during His earthly ministry. Any interpretation that contradicts what Jesus plainly taught in the

Olivet Discourse cannot be the intended meaning of that which He taught in any of the prophetic books of the Bible such as Daniel, Isaiah, Joel, or Revelation.

This book is not intended to rehash the popular, traditional teachings of our day on eschatology, but rather to open up the minds of the readers to explore and consider concepts and views that lie outside of the box of the commonly accepted teachings being taught to this present generation. God's Word declares that some of these prophetic things will be sealed or hidden from man until the last days of this age. However, God promises to reveal that which has been hidden to this last day/terminal generation.

Preface

We are living in a time when the number of views on eschatology are almost as numerous as there are church denominations (slight exaggeration). What is *eschatology*? Webster's dictionary defines it as, "A branch of theology concerned with the final events in the history of the world. It would include various Christian doctrines such as the second coming, the resurrection of the dead, or the last judgment." Simply stated, it is the study of end time events. Of those who share their views on such, most cite the Bible as their source and proof of the very doctrine they espouse.

Why are there so many views if these views are based on the same book? Often, the reason for this is because the biblical view being espoused is not that of the one speaking, but rather the view of what he has heard another articulate. Many Christians simply parrot what they have been taught, assuming it was biblically based, especially if the teacher is well known. Attaching a Scripture to an opinion or view does not necessarily make it a biblical view. Most Christians, even many pastors, are not well-versed and studied on end time events.

Why is it that so few have studied the Scriptures to ascertain what the Bible says about eschatology? Is it because they have been led to believe that eschatology is too deep to understand? Or, is it because they have been taught that it is not really that important in our Christian walk? Whatever the reason might be, the subject of eschatology is avoided by the majority of Christians, even by most pastors. Rarely is the book of Revelation used extensively as a part of the many sermons preached weekly from pulpits. It seems that this last book of the Bible is avoided like the plague. This most likely is the result of pastors not being confident or not feeling comfortable having to deal with the stir and the questions such teachings might generate.

And yet a number of others seem to embrace what is commonly referred to as, "The Pan Theory." These say that if you simply walk daily with Jesus, your eschatology does not matter; it will all "pan" out in the end. To this I would say that eschatology forms two of the six foundational teachings of the doctrine of Christ found in Hebrews 6:1-2. I remind you that Jesus chided the Pharisees and the Sadducees because they did greatly err concerning the doctrine of the resurrection of the dead (see Matthew 22:23-33 and Mark 12:24-27). This doctrine definitely has something to do with eschatology, and we need to be careful lest we, too, greatly err. From this we can conclude that Jesus considered eschatology to be very important to the life and walk of His people. He even taught on it. His teaching on eschatology is recorded in three of the four Gospels. He shared His view with His disciples on the Mount of Olives, and this teaching is commonly referred to as the Olivet Discourse.

Yet another proof of its importance can be seen in 2 Thessalonians 2, written by Paul to the Thessalonians. From this epistle, we can see that Paul charged the Thessalonians to be prepared for the coming of the day of the Lord. Did not the Holy Spirit know that this was unnecessary because the day of the Lord would not happen in their lifetime? I don't think so. Why would Paul teach on it if it were not relevant? I believe Paul knew the importance of having an expectancy of the coming of the Lord to motivate God's people to stay on task. Is it any less important for the church of today to be expectant and vigilant as we continually move closer and closer to the end of this age?

I trust that this book will serve to motivate you to be diligent in searching the Scriptures and inquiring inside the temple for the revelation of God concerning His view on eschatology. God does have a view. He has declared it in the Bible, which must mean that it is important. We certainly would not want to suggest that God would include in the Holy Scriptures things that were not important to His people but rather were simply added as filler material between the pieces of important information. Therefore, it truly is important for all! Remember, all Scripture is profitable for all God's people. Yes, even eschatology is. We have no basis to conclude that the scriptural view of eschatology is only important to a handful of Christians who would be born at the end of this age. Remember, Jesus sharply rebuked the religious people who were not a part of the last days generation for their lack of skill in interpreting the Scriptures concerning this matter. Therefore, may we all be encouraged to study to show ourselves approved unto God, as workmen who do not need to be ashamed. Being ashamed of what? That is, being ashamed of not knowing what was important enough to God to include in our Bibles that we so dearly love and respect.

Acknowledgments

Anytime we accomplish some major feat in our lives, it is important to acknowledge the fact that who we are and what we do is greatly shaped, affected, influenced and, to a great extent, determined by the impact that others have had on our lives. In writing this book, I recognize this fact to be very much a reality. The acknowledgements that follow are not intended to be a complete or exhaustive list of people who have had a major impact on my life but to those who, in particular, most contributed to this project in some way.

First of all, I would like to acknowledge my wife, Paulette. I had the privilege of being married to her for 48+ years before she went to be with the Lord. Her unending support and encouragement to me and the ministry to which God called me made possible what would not have been possible without her. Although I did not start writing this book until after she passed away, the vast majority of what I wrote had been determined and thoroughly discussed with her on many occasions. She often served as my revelational sounding board and chief encourager in my pursuit of God's truth. I miss her greatly!

Next I want to acknowledge my son Jason as well as Bruce Ekern who both serve with me on the pastoral staff of our church,

New Life Christian Center. We have literally spent countless hours discussing and sharing personal views with one another concerning eschatology and a vast array of many other biblical doctrines. Their research and insights have indeed been invaluable.

Next I want to acknowledge three of my dearest and long-standing friends. The longest relationship (70 years) is with my natural and spiritual brother, Ron King. Then there is George Barrett, a faithful friend of 44 years, and Roger Pugh, a faithful friend of 39 years. Together we co-labored in ministry for many years and founded and/or served as directors of Apostolic Team Ministries International (ATM), which is an apostolic network of ministries and churches both domestic and international. It has truly been an honor and a lifeline to have such friends with whom I have had the privilege to minister alongside these many years. Not only am I grateful for the countless ministry trips together but also for the countless hours of discussing, even debating, the doctrines of the faith. Often these discussions and sharing of insights lasted into the early hours of the morning. The insights gleaned from these times together have had a major influence in the writing of *The Terminal Generation*.

And last but not least of all, I want to acknowledge Jesus, my Lord, my Savior, and my best friend by whom and from whom all true revelation comes, whether it be firsthand or secondhand. First Corinthians 4:6b-7 serves to remind me to maintain a proper perspective in both sharing and receiving revelation with all lowliness and meekness of mind.

> **[6]...that you may learn in us not to think beyond what is written, that none of you may be puffed up on behalf of one against the other. [7]For who makes you differ from**

another? And what do you have that you did not receive? Now if you did indeed receive it, why do you boast as if you had not received it?   —1 Corinthians 4:6-7

Thank You, Jesus!

And thank you all!

Section One:

What Jesus Taught on Eschatology from the Earth

1

In the Beginning

Introduction to the Study

It is important to know that before God laid the foundations of this world, God had a plan and a goal to be attained in it. His plan and goal can be clearly seen by looking at the account of creation. Shortly after He created this world, He planted a garden east of Eden. The quality of life in this garden was superior to the quality of life in the rest of the earth. The Garden of Eden was not created by God but rather was planted by God after creation as a seed in God's field, the earth. In this garden, we see the intersection of two worlds, the created spiritual world and the created natural world (Colossians 1:16-17). It was, in fact, the intersection of the kingdom of God and this natural world in one small corner of the earth. This intersection or the combining of two worlds can be evidenced by taking note of the fact that there were both natural beings and spiritual beings living there. There were also natural trees and spiritual trees growing there. God gave man, not the devil, dominion to rule over the earth. This was to be accomplished by filling it through fruitfulness and multiplication of mankind created in the image of God. However, God made it clear that Adam would have to subdue it and take authority over it. Later, when God was speaking to Moses, He restated His purpose for the earth. He said that He wanted the whole earth to be filled with His glory and, as surely as God lives, He would see to it that it came to pass. This could only happen by taking the quality of life resulting from the intersection of the kingdom of God and God's natural earth to the four corners of this earth.

For 6,000 years, God has waited patiently for His purpose and goal to be accomplished in this earth. Man has failed to accomplish his God-given role in bringing this to pass. However, God will see His purpose fulfilled as He works through man in the last 1,000 years or the seventh millennium. This is commonly referred to as the millennial kingdom. I believe we are living in a time when the saints who are here on this earth will close out one age and usher in a new one. I believe many alive today will be a part of the terminal generation of this age.

As we draw near to the end of this age, it is important for us to prepare and position ourselves to advance His kingdom. Why? Because our task of filling the earth with the glory of the kingdom of God is destined to happen in the midst of extreme adversarial conditions as prophetically set forth in the Scriptures. The charge given to man in the very beginning could not be accomplished without man subduing and taking dominion. This infers a warning from God that there would be resistance to the God-given commission. Adam failed this commission in his day, but for those of us charged to fulfill it in our day, nothing has changed. Neither the commission nor the resistance, which is hell-bent on foiling the plan God destined to be fulfilled through and by man, has changed. It is important for us to realize that the resistance is spiritual in nature. It resulted from eating of a spiritual tree, the tree of the knowledge of good and evil. Instead of subduing and taking dominion over the devil in the garden, man's dominion to rule was both abdicated by Adam and usurped by the devil. Because of Jesus, the last Adam, God's Great Commission will be fulfilled as all the kingdoms of this world will be subjugated and put under the feet of God and His kingdom. It will be the best of times; it will be the worst of times ... best for the church and worst for the world and the kingdom of darkness.

Four Mindsets

For this reason, a study of eschatology may be more important than many Christians think. Before undertaking this study, I want to state four positions that represent the mindsets of most Christians concerning eschatology. I do this that you might decide which mindset best represents your current thinking. I'm only using four positions. There may be others that would more accurately identify the position you currently embrace as well as what you are sensing about the times in which you are living. Take a moment to consider with which of these four you most closely identify.

1. I sense the imminent return of Christ any day now.

2. I believe we are in the last days but certain events must come to pass before Christ can return.

3. I do not sense Christ's soon return and it could be many years before His coming.

4. I do not believe in a literal second coming of Christ and a catching up of His church since the saints of God will usher in the kingdom of God without His return.

Guidelines for Section One

Now that we have somewhat located ourselves concerning eschatology, I want to discuss the general guidelines we will implement in the two sections of this book. Section One of this book, *What Jesus Taught on Eschatology from the Earth*, will focus on what Jesus taught His disciples concerning eschatology during His earthly ministry. Section Two of this book, *What Jesus Taught on Eschatology from Heaven*, will focus on what Jesus taught concerning eschatology from heaven to those on this earth, such as the apostles and prophets of both the Old and New Testaments.

In Section One, we want to operate on a "what if" premise. The premise is, "What if there were no other Scriptures in all of the Bible dealing with the subject of eschatology except what He taught on the Mount of Olives recorded in the gospels of Matthew, Mark, and Luke. What truth could we learn and know about the inevitable eschatological events God has predetermined on this earth even before its foundations were laid?" Should not the events and timeline of both the earthly and heavenly accounts of eschatology be the same? What Jesus taught from heaven will never disagree with what He taught on the earth.

Eschatology is something that many people are interested in. There are so many varied positions, but I want to try to keep it simple. It is my primary purpose not to present any particular bent, position, or opinion concerning eschatology in this section of the book. I simply want to look at what Jesus taught His disciples while He was with them on the earth. For the most part, I am not going to use any other prophetic books, such as Isaiah or Zechariah or Hosea or Daniel, or even Revelation, the last book of the Bible.

When studying eschatology, the thing that often makes it difficult and confusing is that the scholar approaches it from a topical viewpoint. This approach attempts to find and then glean from the entirety of the Scriptures all that pertains to the vast subject of eschatology. It is not an easy task to form one's position using this approach.

Understanding what the prophets of old have spoken is indeed a difficult task. Often, even the prophets who spoke did not understand that which they were prophesying. A classic example of this would be Caiaphas, the high priest at the time of Jesus' death. From his office of high priest, he accurately prophesied the Word of God. He prophetically declared by the Spirit that it was both the will of God and expedient that one should die for the nation. See this Scripture:

> [47]Then the chief priests and the Pharisees gathered a council and said, "What shall we do? For this Man works many signs. [48]If we let Him alone like this, everyone will believe in Him, and the Romans will come and take away both our place and nation." [49]And one of them, Caiaphas, being high priest that year, said to them, "You know nothing at all, [50]nor do you consider that it is expedient for us that one man should die for the people, and not that the whole nation should perish." [51]Now this he did not say on his own authority; but being high priest that year he prophesied that Jesus would die for the nation, [52]and not for that nation only, but also that He would gather together in one the children of God who were scattered abroad. —John 11:47-52

He did not know he was prophesying about Jesus. As a matter of fact, Jesus was brought before him and condemned by the very high priest who uttered the prophecy.

In this section we will use an expository teaching approach. An expository approach is a verse-by-verse study of a portion of Scripture. Another reason for this approach is that the Bible only records one time where Jesus taught extensively on the subject of eschatology during His earthly ministry. This teaching is commonly referred to as the Olivet Discourse. The Olivet Discourse is found in three of the four gospel accounts – Matthew, Mark, and Luke. Only John does not record Jesus' eschatological teaching that was spoken on the Mount of Olives. John, the apostle whom Jesus loved, did weigh in on what Jesus taught eschatologically in the last book of the Bible, Revelation. The apostle John was caught up into the third heaven long after Christ's ascension to receive this revelation. Consequently, John does not share what Jesus taught from the earth but rather what He taught from heaven. However, John did have the privilege of hearing what Jesus taught on this subject both on the earth and from heaven. There should be no doubt in the heart of any believer that these teachings would be in total agreement, especially since both are recorded in the Scriptures. In Section One of this book, our scriptural focus will be limited almost entirely to the Olivet Discourse and, even more specifically, to the Matthew 24 account.

An Important Question to Ask Ourselves

Before we begin our study, let us consider and meditate on an important question. The question is, "Does the Bible indicate that all Christians need to prepare for the last days or only those who will be alive in the last days?" If your answer is, "Only those who will be alive in the last days," then answer, why it is that Paul taught the Thessalonians to prepare for the day of the Lord? Did the Holy Spirit not know that these Christians would not be alive in the last days? If your answer is, "All Christians throughout all ages need to prepare," then should it not be of extreme importance to know for what we are to prepare? With that in mind, let us begin our study of what Jesus taught on eschatology while on this earth. It is more important than many Christians and even Christian leaders are willing to acknowledge. This is clearly seen in the latter when we take note of how seldom the last book of the Bible is incorporated into their Sunday morning sermons. Knowing about the last times could make a difference between being a victor in the coming spiritual warfare or being a casualty thereof. Remember, Paul gave warning to Timothy about the perilous times that would come in the last days (2 Timothy 3:1). In taking heed to this warning, let us begin our study with an open heart. Let us too be noble like the Bereans, searching the Scriptures to see if the things being said are true. This may require you temporarily laying aside any preconceived notions or positions on this very important subject in order to objectively examine the merits of what is being said.

Two Types of Scriptural Fulfillments

It is especially important before beginning to deal with eschatology that we understand how God brings about the fulfillment of predictive Scriptures. Often predictive or prophetic Scriptures have more than one fulfillment. When these fulfillments occur, they happen literally. There can be one or more typological prophetic fulfillments, which we will term a *literal typological prophetic*

fulfillment. However, there can only be one ultimate prophetic fulfillment, which we will term the *literal ultimate prophetic fulfillment.*

Let me give you an example of what I am talking about. The
tabernacle of Moses, the tabernacle of David, Solomon's temple,
the rebuilt temple, and Herod's temple were all literal yet typological fulfillments of an ultimate prophetic intention of God. They
were types and shadows of something very real, conceived of in
the heart of God. Though these types and shadows are not the
ultimate consummation of the real, they point to and give a partial
picture of the God-conceived reality. Though these shadows reveal
some of what God has conceived in His heart, only the body or
object that cast the shadow can ultimately reveal the fullness of the
God-conceived reality.

In the case of the various tabernacles and temples, they were
types and shadows that prophetically pointed to the true temple
of God made without man's hands. These were all pointing to
a temple made of living stones whose architect, foundation, and
builder was God alone.

Another example of this multiple fulfillment principle can be
seen in the predictive Scriptures prophesying of the coming of
one who would be the Messiah, the Redeemer, and the Savior
of mankind. These prophecies were given many years before the
reality of them actually happened. Looking back, we now know
that Jesus was the ultimate consummation of these Scriptures.
However, there were several literal yet typological fulfillments of
this prophetic promise of God. Abraham, Joseph, and Moses were
types and shadows of the body that cast their shadows. The body
that cast their shadows was none other than Jesus, the true Messiah, Redeemer, and Savior.

¹⁶Let no man therefore judge you in meat, or in drink, or in respect of an holyday, or of the new moon, or of the sabbath days: ¹⁷which are a shadow of things to come; but the body is of Christ.   —Colossians 2:16-17 KJV

Before concluding this principle, let me give one other example of a *literal typological prophetic fulfillment* and the *literal ultimate prophetic fulfillment* from the Scriptures.

¹For the law, having a shadow of the good things to come, and not the very image of the things, can never with these same sacrifices, which they offer continually year by year, make those who approach perfect.   —Hebrews 10:1

This Scripture declares that the law of Moses or the Old Testament was just a typological fulfillment of something greater to come. It was only a shadow which was to serve as a hint or picture of the body that cast this shadow. Later on in this same passage of Scripture, the body which cast this shadow of the greater thing to come was identified. It had to do with where the law of God was written as well as with a person. In the Old Testament the law was written on stone, but in the New Testament the law of God was written on the hearts of God's people. The One who was sacrificed for sin and sat down at the right hand of God was none other than Jesus Christ.

¹¹And every priest stands ministering daily and offering repeatedly the same sacrifices, which can never take away sins. ¹²But this Man, after He had offered one sacrifice for sins forever, sat down at the right hand of God, ¹³from that time waiting till His enemies are made His footstool. ¹⁴For by one offering He has perfected forever those who are being sanctified. ¹⁵But the

Holy Spirit also witnesses to us; for after He had said before, ¹⁶"This is the covenant that I will make with them after those days, says the Lord: I will put My laws into their hearts, and in their minds I will write them."   —Hebrews 10:11-16

The Old Testament, or the law of Moses, is an example of the term this author has coined as a *literal typological prophetic fulfillment*. The New Testament, or the law of the spirit of life in Christ Jesus (God's law written on man's heart), is an example of the term this author has coined as the *literal ultimate prophetic fulfillment*.

The literal ultimate fulfillment/interpretation of Acts 1:8 is not limited to Jerusalem or Judea but to the entire world. That is a typological fulfillment pointing to an ultimate prophetic reality that would occur at the end of the age.

The *literal ultimate prophetic fulfillment* interpretation of Pentecost in Acts 2 goes beyond just Jewish Christians receiving the baptism of the Holy Spirit. The *literal ultimate prophetic fulfillment* of Joel 2 declares that the Holy Spirit was to be poured out on all flesh, not just Jewish flesh as on the day of Pentecost.

In studying the doctrine of eschatology, it is important to understand and employ this principle of the two types of predictive, scriptural fulfillments. And now, let us begin our study of what Jesus taught while on this earth concerning the subject of eschatology.

2

Introduction and Signs 1 & 2 of End Times

The Audience

As we begin our expository study of Matthew 24, we first want to determine the audience to whom Jesus was teaching. Was it to sinners or to religious people who were natural Israelites, or to believing Jews? In Matthew 24:1 it is clearly stated that His target audience was His own believing disciples. This teaching was not to all the people of Israel; it was directed toward those who knew Him relationally and whose names were written in the Lamb's Book of Life. These disciples represent the very firstfruits or members of the New Testament church that He was building. It was not given to Jews, nationally speaking or naturally speaking, but it was given to a people who were truly Jews or Israelites internally. See these verses from Romans 2:

> 28For he is not a Jew who is one outwardly, nor is circumcision that which is outward in the flesh; 29but he is a

Jew who is one inwardly; and circumcision is that of the heart, in the Spirit, not in the letter; whose praise is not from men but from God.   —Romans 2:28-29

The Backdrop

Matthew 24 verses 1 and 2 clearly depict the context that inspired this teaching by Jesus. He and His disciples were leaving the temple in Jerusalem when His disciples began to point out the beauty and majesty of the temple (Luke 21:5). Jesus, knowing that this was the last time He would ever set foot in this temple, began to prophesy about its destruction. He told them that so utterly complete would be the destruction that there would not be one stone left on top of another. This news had to be both shocking and disturbing to His disciples. It generated questions in their hearts and minds, you can be sure. So much so that they seized the first opportunity when they were alone with Jesus on the Mount of Olives to pose some questions concerning His comments.

The Three Questions

Wanting to know more about that which Jesus had just spoken, they privately asked Him three questions:

1. When will the destruction of the temple happen?

2. What shall be the sign of your coming?

3. What will be the signs of the end of this age?

It is important to remember that when you have more than one gospel account sharing the same story, you need to look at all the parts in all the gospels and consolidate them to get a more complete picture of what was being said. Only the passage found in Luke 21 records Jesus' answer to the first question. Though Jesus did not give a specific timetable for the destruction of the temple, He did give great detail of specific events and living conditions just prior to the destruction of Jerusalem and the temple. From history, we know that Jesus was referencing the destruction of Jerusalem and the temple in 70 AD. Jesus prophesied this destruction, however, before it was history.

The Signs of the End of This Age

In Matthew 24:4, Jesus began to address the third question, concerning the signs preceding and leading up to the end of the age. Some Bible translations may say "the end of the world" instead of "the end of the age." That would be a different question entirely and would be represented by different signs and a different time period. The Greek word used in this verse is *aion,* which means "age" or "a period of time" or even speaks of eternal things. The Greek word for "world" is *cosmos.* So the question asked was, "Tell us the sign of the end of the age."

I personally believe the age of man is 6,000 years, which God has given man to fulfill the Commission which He gave Adam in the garden. I believe it can be broken into three 2,000-year periods. From Adam to Isaac, the Child of Promise, is 2,000 years; from Isaac to Jesus' first coming is 2,000 years; from Jesus' first coming to Jesus' second coming is 2,000 years. The seventh 1,000-year period is the millennial kingdom. This is the seventh day or the seventh 1,000-year period during which man will rest from his labors to fulfill his God-given commission. It will be a time when we co-labor with God in His cultivated field, the earth. It will truly be a "co-mission" between God and man. Yes, it will truly be a time when God's mission to fill the whole earth with His glory will become a living reality.

The First Sign

Now, let us get back to the signs that will precede and lead up to the culmination of this present age. Jesus begins to respond to question three in Matthew 24:4. The very first words out of His mouth were, "Take heed that no one deceive you." Jesus was warning His disciples that the very first sign that would initiate the steady march toward the end of the age would be spiritual deception. It is interesting to note that *to take heed* means "to discern by paying attention with the senses," "to be on the look," or "to listen by keeping your ear to the ground." Jesus is telling His people that He wants us to know these things and that He is going to have certain signs and events take place to let us know where we are in His prophetic timetable. He gives us signs so that we won't be taken by surprise in that day, like children of the night. After all, He refers to us as children of the day or light.

Do you remember what was said about the sons of the tribe of Issachar as to how they were gifted? Their particular gifting was the knowledge given to them by God of the seasons and times in which they were living and what they should do in those seasons and times. They had an ability to know just where they were in God's prophetic timetable. Likewise, Jesus was willing to divulge specific signs to His disciples, both then and throughout the age, that they might know what to take heed to as the end of the age approaches.

That word *deceive* in Matthew 24:4 means "to cause one to err" or "to cause one to be seduced and consequently moved from a place of safety." This is what Jesus said is going to happen. How will it happen? Matthew 24:5 says that many will come in the Lord's name saying I am the Christ and will deceive many. Do you really think it would fool you if some man came up to you and said, "By the way, I am Jesus, the Christ?" How many others do you think would be deceived by that? What was Jesus referring to, then? The word in the Greek for "Christ" is *christos* which means "the anointed one" or "one who carries the anointing." There have been many teachers who have stood before God's people since Christ's ascension and declared that they were anointed by God and that what they were saying was by the anointing. With some of these, there will even be signs and wonders accompanying their ministries, which will cause many to exclaim, "Wow, they must really be plugged in to God! They couldn't do these things unless they were sent by God from heaven and God was with them." Sounds like something Nicodemus would say.

> [1]There was a man of the Pharisees named Nicodemus, a ruler of the Jews. [2]This man came to Jesus by night and said to Him, "Rabbi, we know that You are a teacher come from God; for no one can do these signs that You do unless God is with him.   —John 3:1-2

We should all know that there can be signs and wonders from both teams. The devil counterfeits everything that has worked for Jesus. Of this fact there is no doubt. The goal of both teams in manifesting signs and wonders is to validate themselves and their agendas as being from God. Jesus taught that it is not by their signs, wonders, or gifts that you would know those who are His, but by their fruit. Here Jesus is exhorting His people to be on guard for deception, not by sinners but from those professing to be spiritual. Remember, Judas Iscariot did signs and wonders. The safety is in being a fruit inspector, not a signs and wonders inspector. This is how you can tell the difference between false and true apostles, false and true prophets, and false and true brothers.

I believe that the sign of deception began to rear its ugly head through the spirit of antichrist sometime after the destruction of Jerusalem and the temple in 70 AD and before John wrote his first epistle in 95 AD. In his first epistle, John states that though there will be a literal Antichrist, there were already many antichrists in the churches. But because of the anointing, they were exposed and left the churches.

> [18]Little children, it is the last hour; and as you have heard that the Antichrist is coming, even now many antichrists have come, by which we know that it is the last hour. [19]They went out from us, but they were not of us; for if they had been of us, they would have continued with us; but they went out that they might be made manifest, that none of them were of us. [20]But you have an anointing from the Holy One, and you know all things.
>
> —1 John 2:18-20

We must understand that the spirit of antichrist is not necessarily anti-Jesus. Many of these professed Jesus but were still antichrists because they were anti-true anointing. John's assertion was that the true anointing guards against the deception of a false anointing.

> [26]These things I have written to you concerning those who try to deceive you. [27]But the anointing which you have received from Him abides in you, and you do not need that anyone teach you; but as the same anointing teaches you concerning all things, and is true, and is not a

lie, and just as it has taught you, you will abide in Him.
—1 John 2:26-27

As we move closer to the end of this age, the number of religious impostors will increase. As a matter of fact, Matthew 24:5 says that many of these deceivers will come in Jesus' name. These will say they believe in and love Jesus but then teach and tolerate things that Jesus would never endorse. Not only will their numbers increase but also so will the audience they influence. I believe this will be made possible largely because of their availability to people through the latest and greatest media venues such as the Internet and, in particular, YouTube, where anyone can pass themselves off as an expert. It is hard to test the fruit of a person's life through the Internet.

The Second Sign

In Matthew 24:6, Jesus says the next thing you need to watch for is that you will hear of wars and rumors of wars. One might ask the question, "Haven't there always been wars and rumors of wars?" The obvious answer to that is, "Yes, throughout the history of mankind there has always been wars and rumors of wars." If that is true, what was Jesus talking about in this Scripture? Jesus was speaking of signs that would have a universal or worldwide impact. If the gospel is to be preached to the entire world, then God intended it to apply to the entire world. An example of what I am talking about would be that when there was a war between England and France, it basically only affected England and France. This war did not affect countries like India, China, or Egypt. Therefore that war would not be indicative of the sign Jesus was talking about, since its impact was not global. You can be sure that the end of this age will have a global affect, as will the signs that precede it. It is not until near the end of the sixth millennium that there was a war that affected the entire world. I don't mean to infer everybody was fighting in it, but it had such widespread ramifications that it affected the economy or geopolitical environments of the entire world. Its affect was global and that's why they called it World War I. If that wasn't enough, approximately 25 years later there was another, which was called World War II. Since then we have had Korea, Vietnam, Iraq, Afghanistan; now rumors of even bigger, more impacting wars loom on the horizon.

As we continue looking at Matthew 24:6, we see that Jesus made a very interesting and profound statement. In the first half of the verse He tells us what sign we are to be looking for, whereas in the second half He tells us not to be troubled, terrified, or alarmed when we see it because it is not a sign of the end. He said that these first two things must come to pass, but the end is not yet. However, many Christians during World War I and World War II began to teach that Jesus is coming any moment now. It seems that any time things get really bad, the rhetoric of many becomes apocalyptic and frantic. The problem is, they did not heed the entirety of this verse. He says that when you see the deception, the wars, and the rumors of war, don't be perplexed, don't be terrified. Why? For all these things must come to pass, but the end is not yet. These things have nothing, and I repeat nothing, to do with end time events. These first two signs are in reality just precursors to the signs of the end times.

In the next chapter, we will begin to discuss the signs that are truly signs of the last days.

3

Signs 3 & 4 of End Times

The Third Sign

God's instruction to His people after the first two signs was not to be alarmed or frightened, because other things had to first come to pass before the unfolding of the last days began. In Matthew 24:7, Jesus begins to describe some of the other events that have to take place before the end of the age comes. He said that nation shall rise against nation, kingdom against kingdom, and there will be famines, pestilences, and earthquakes in various places. I believe the third sign is competition between nations and kingdoms. With regard to nation against nation, this is not actual war, as that would be a repeating of the second sign. I believe this is referring to cold wars where nations are continually strategizing against one another to gain superiority or even supremacy over the other. This has been happening on a global scale since World War II. There is even competition amongst nations who are allies. In other words, we want the dollar to be stronger than the pound even though England is one of our closest allies. We still rejoice when our dollar makes inroads against their pound. And do you think England is sad when the dollar falls and the pound rises? No, we all rejoice secretly over the other's loss and our gain. All of this is to gain economical, political, social, and/or military advantage over the other.

However, Matthew 24:7 goes on to say that not only shall nation rise against nation, but also kingdom shall rise against kingdom. I believe that kingdom against kingdom is meant to be a contrast to nation against nation rather than a mere repetition. Kingdom against kingdom speaks of warfare and competition between spiritual kingdoms. I believe Jesus is talking about the kingdom of darkness rising up against the kingdom of light, or the kingdom of God against the kingdom of the devil.

I was born during World War II and have seen this phenomenon actually happen. As a young lad growing up, the devil's tactic was to make people believe that he wasn't real or didn't exist. Even Hollywood portrayed him as an evil influence and not a real being. Throughout my life I began to see a change, even in Hollywood. The devil has come out of the closet. He no longer wants people to view him as a myth but rather as a real being. He seduces people in order to align them with him by offering them power to attain a better life and to control the lives of others through the spirit of witchcraft. He openly declares that he has more power and a better deal than what God is offering. Hollywood is one of his biggest allies, ginning up such interest and preoccupation with the likes of Harry Potter, Twilight, and other paranormal productions. When you factor in their continual promotion of the agendas of gays/lesbians, graphic violence, blatant sexuality, and the dismantling of the family unit and family values as we have known them for centuries, it is no wonder that there is such animosity between the kingdom of light and the kingdom of darkness. Oh, and let us not forget the agendas of humanism, secularism, and anti-religion! As a result of this animus, the most discriminated against group of people today is not the blacks; it is not the Hispanics; it is not the gays; it is born-again Christians. Most people would have never imagined this happening in the United States, which was founded and based upon Christian principles, but it has. Consider some of the criteria by which this government now defines a radical terrorist. They are those who believe that Jesus Christ is coming again to rapture or catch away born-again believers to be with Him throughout all eternity. They believe in a literal return of Jesus Christ. Many of them are into home schooling. Even the Muslims are protected and have more freedoms in this country, which is evidenced by the fact that the government is more concerned about not offending Muslims than they are about offending Christians.

Saints of God, wake up and heed these signs of which Jesus warned. Kingdom is rising against kingdom. There is such animus between the kingdoms of light and darkness, yet many Christians are succumbing to this sinister agenda under the guise of being more tolerant. Many religious folks espouse that there are many names for God, but it's the same God. They say we just need to get along with each other and stop being so narrow-minded and intolerant. The Word of God says that there is no other name under heaven by which man can be saved than that name which is Jesus. If we are going to believe these warning signs, let us remember who the author of them is. He is the One who says that there is no other name and no other way to God except through Jesus. Yes, the way is narrow and, yes, God will not tolerate any other name to attain the salvation of God.

The Fourth Sign

I personally believe that one of the consequences of the clashing of both natural dominions and spiritual dominions will precipitate severe judgments similar to the judgments God prophesied of in Ezekiel 5:17. Knowing the truth of God's immutability (unchangeableness) should also cause one to know that similar conditions result in similar judgments. We have Bible precedence of man's ability to pollute nature (the cause of the flood) and the devil's ability to pervert nature (the cause of the tornado that killed Job's children). In Matthew 24:7 Jesus confirms this by saying that after a period of time in which nation shall rise against nation and kingdom against kingdom, there will follow such things as famines, pestilences, and earthquakes throughout the entirety of the inhabited places. It is interesting to note that the word for earthquake in the Greek can refer to an earthquake or an upheaval or turmoil amongst people. Not only is the earth's nature convulsing and reacting to all the ungodliness, but there are also major upheavals and tremors socially, economically, politically, and spiritually. Wow, does this not describe much of what we are experiencing in this present world? Indeed, God says that before the end comes, nation shall rise against nation, kingdom shall rise against kingdom, there shall be famines, pestilences, upheavals, turmoil, and death to such a degree that the entire world will reel under its impact. Also, the Luke account adds to these signs that fearful sights and great signs shall happen in the heavens. These are more than random shooting stars or an occasional meteor shower. These shall be of such a magnitude that people will be terrified, not just because the heavens are in danger but because of the danger they pose to the earth.

God's direction to His people concerning the first two signs was to look for them but not to be alarmed by them when they happen. They are not indicators of the end, just precursors. His instruction, however, concerning the last two signs covered in Matthew 24 is different. He says that when you observe these signs, you are to look at these as the beginning of sorrows. The Greek word for *sorrows* in Matthew 24:8 is "Odin," which means "birth pains" or "the travail of childbirth." Birth pains precede something new being birthed into our midst. Once they start, something new, unique, and never before seen is inevitably on the way. Remember these birth pains; we will come back to discuss these again later in this book. These are the beginning of something that bears much significance in God's prophetic timetable at the end of this age.

4

Before Any Signs Begin

Answering Question 1

The first question Jesus' disciples asked Him was about the timing of the destruction of the temple in Jerusalem. As we stated earlier, only the account in the gospel of Luke answers this question. As we compare the account in Luke with the accounts in Matthew and Mark, they track almost identically. All four signs that we covered in the previous chapters of this book are also in the Luke account. It is not until you get to Luke 21:12 that you see a difference. In the very first words of verse 12, Jesus makes a very important statement. Jesus, in referencing the four previous signs, said that before all of these signs happen, something else would happen. We read:

> ¹²But before all these things, they will lay their hands on you and persecute you, delivering you up to the synagogues and prisons. You will be brought before kings and rulers for My name's sake.   —Luke 21:12

Signs Before the Signs

There are a number of things to learn from Luke 21:12. First of all, Jesus is directing His comments not to natural Israel but to believers or spiritual Israel. He tells them that the authorities are going to lay hands on them, persecute them, and deliver them up to synagogues and into prisons for His namesake. These are Jews who were believers in Jesus, not just Jews by nationality. The religious Jews of that day refused to identify with the name of Jesus. They felt that He was the leader of a cult. The religious leaders of that day said they would allow His disciples to preach anything they wanted; they even could heal the sick and minister to the people, just so long as they didn't do it in the name of Jesus. They threatened to imprison them or to execute them if they did. Many Christians were brought into synagogues to be judged for their failure to comply with the Judeo orthodoxy of that day. The leaders of the synagogues charged them with crimes of treason. They even sent them before kings and rulers because they were followers of Jesus and consequently posed a threat to the Jewish and Roman societies. Jesus encouraged them to not think ahead of time how they would respond to the religious and governmental authorities when they were being tried, but rather that they should depend on God to put the words in their mouths when needed. He promised to give them words of wisdom that would astound their accusers. He went on to tell them that they would be betrayed even by parents, brothers, relatives, and friends, causing many of them to be put to death for Jesus' namesake. Many Christians in the early church were killed. Stephen and James were murdered. The apostle Paul was responsible for much of the suffering of the saints in the early beginnings of the New Testament church. He was even involved in the death of Stephen. Jesus told them that they would be the most persecuted and discriminated against people in the land. Jesus also made it known to them that He was allowing this that they might be a testimony to Him and a witness for the gospel. He encouraged them to be patient and possess their souls through the endurance of sufferings at the hands of their own kinfolk and countrymen.

Then in Luke 21:20, He told them that in the midst of this season of suffering they were to look for a particular sign. He also told them what to do when they saw it. The sign they were to look for was Jerusalem being surrounded by armies. This sign actually was the answer to question number one, "When will the destruction of the temple happen?" He told them that when they saw Jerusalem surrounded by armies, then know that its desolation was near. He went on to say that these were the days of vengeance, that all things which are written may be fulfilled. Why vengeance against His own people who continually cried out for a Messiah to deliver them from the Roman tyranny? It might be because God not only sent them a Messiah in answer to their prayers but also a prophet to introduce His arrival. John 1:11 testifies that the Messiah came unto His own and His own received Him not. Yes, this was judgment against a nation for rejecting their Messiah and missing the day of their visitation. See the Scripture below:

> [41]Now as He drew near, He saw the city and wept over it, [42]saying, "If you had known, even you, especially in this your day, the things that make for your peace! But now they are hidden from your eyes. [43]For days will come upon you when your enemies will build an embankment around you, surround you and close you in on every side, [44]and level you, and your children within you, to the

ground; and they will not leave in you one stone upon
another, because you did not know the time of your visitation."   —Luke 19:41-44

This literally was fulfilled in 70 AD. He specifically instructed
them to leave the city and go to the mountains and not enter the
city again when they saw this sign. Jesus goes on to prophesy that
the nation of Israel would fall by the edge of the sword and be
led away captive into all the nations of the world. History records
that Emperor Titus came and ransacked not only the temple but
also the city of Jerusalem, killing 1.1 million Jews. He took all the
Jewish people and scattered them to the four corners of the earth.
They literally broke up homes and families. This was done to take
away Israel's national identity so that they would never again be
a nation and pose a threat to the empire. In His teaching, Jesus
said that the city of Jerusalem would be trodden down by the
Gentiles until the times of the Gentiles would be fulfilled. Though
the intention of the Roman Empire was to so utterly scatter Israel
throughout the world that their national identity would forever
be lost, God through the Scriptures made clear His intention. He
prophesied that the nation of Israel would once again be gathered
out of all the nations of the world and brought back to the very
land promised to Abraham. History tells us that in 1948 Israel
once again became a nation and was brought back to the very land
from which they were taken captive. However the city of Jerusalem at that time was still in the hands of the Gentiles. During the
Six-Day War of 1967 Israel regained control of Jerusalem. It is
written in the Scriptures that Israel will never be displaced from
their land again and that the city will never fall completely again
into the hands of the Gentiles. From that time forward, I believe
this world has been on a course to transition from the times of

the Gentiles back to the times of the Jews. It is prophesied that the seventh millennium will be the time of the Jews. They and their city, Jerusalem, will be the focal point of life in those days. However, transitions are not immediate; they involve a process. For example, when Samuel anointed David to be king, he was not fully recognized as king over the entire nation until some 15 years later.

Like David, I believe we are in a period of transition where the age of the Gentiles is coming to an end and the age of Israel will begin. It has been in progress since 1967. Remember in Matthew 24:8, Jesus described the third and fourth signs as the beginning of birth pains, more commonly referred to today as labor pains. You may not be able to know the hour or even the day of the birth, but you know that when these start to happen, that which is new and long awaited is definitely on the way. What do they call the time when the baby is between the womb and the world? If you are asking a woman in the throes of childbirth, her answer would probably be, "Pain!!!" However, the doctors and nurses would say, "She's in transition."

If we would just take a few moments to consider what we have seen since the two world wars have ended, it would stagger us. We've seen Israel become a nation; we've seen Jerusalem restored to Israel; we've seen nations rise against nations and kingdoms against kingdoms; we've seen a drastic increase in the number of earthquakes; we've seen drastic changes in our weather patterns which have caused famines; we've seen pestilences; we've seen new mysterious diseases; we've even seen great and fearful signs in the heavens. I believe these provide very persuasive evidence that would lead one to conclude that the birth pains have begun and that we are now in a time of transition. If we factor in the fact that

Jesus exhorted His people in Luke 21:28 that when these things *begin* to come to pass, we are to look up for our redemption draws near. Look at what He also says in the following verses:

> ²⁹Then He spoke to them a parable: "Look at the fig tree, and all the trees. ³⁰When they are already budding, you see and know for yourselves that summer is now near. ³¹So you also, when you see these things happening, know that the kingdom of God is near. ³²Assuredly, I say to you, this generation will by no means pass away till all things take place. ³³Heaven and earth will pass away, but My words will by no means pass away.
>
> —Luke 21:29-33

Don't allow yourselves to be lulled asleep by the endless chatter of those who mockingly say that Christian alarmists have been preaching this tired old message for years and years to frighten people. We have plenty of time left; we are headed for a time of peace and safety. We just need to draw together and strive for world peace.

On the contrary, we need to harken to the words of Jesus to His church in the last days. He admonished His children to awake from their slumber so that day would not, like a snare, take them by surprise. He instructed that we watch and pray, that we might be counted worthy to escape all these things.

> ³⁴"But take heed to yourselves, lest your hearts be weighed down with carousing, drunkenness, and cares of this life, and that Day come on you unexpectedly. ³⁵For it will come as a snare on all those who dwell on the face of the whole earth. ³⁶Watch therefore, and pray always that you may be counted worthy to escape all these things that

will come to pass, and to stand before the Son of Man."
—Luke 21:34-36

A question that each individual must ask himself at this juncture is, "Do I see any evidence that the events that are described as
the beginning of birth pains in Matthew 24:8 have already begun
to take place?" If we answer in the affirmative, then our instruction is clear and we must be about our Father's business.

5

Sign 5 and the Great Tribulation

Reviewing the First Four Signs

Now that we have covered Jesus' answer to the first question the disciples asked, let us resume answering the two questions concerning the signs of the end of this age. I am referring specifically to the questions, "What shall be the sign of Your coming?" and "What shall be the sign of the end of the age?" For didactic purposes, I have broken down these signs into seven events and/or groups of events.

Jesus said the very first sign was going to be deception. Deception is going to be at an all-time high the closer we get to the end of the age. I believe shortly after 70 AD there was a deceiving spirit loosed on this earth called the spirit of antichrist. This spirit has gone forth to conquer through deception. This spirit has primarily operated through religious people, many of who were faithful to attend local churches. This is still the case even at this present hour. The spirit of antichrist has been busy cultivating a culture of deception that will pave the way for the coming of and the receiving of the literal Antichrist.

Jesus said the second sign was wars and rumors of wars. Like all of the signs at the end of the age, these wars will have a universal affect and global impact. I believe this sign is in direct reference to the two world wars and the many threats of war since.

Jesus said the third sign would be that nation would rise against nation and kingdom against kingdom. I believe this sign amongst nations is in direct reference to the cold wars and international competition that has been prevalent since the close of World War II. I believe kingdom against kingdom is in reference to the intensifying onslaught of the kingdom of darkness against the kingdom of light.

Jesus said the fourth sign indicates that there would be famines, pestilences, and earthquakes in various places. In the Hebrew language the word *ka tah'* means "more than various." It carries the connotation of being throughout and beyond measure. This seems to infer that all three of these disasters will be throughout the world or in many places even to the point of being so numerous that they are beyond measure.

Jesus said in Matthew 24:8 that all those things listed in the third and fourth signs would be the beginning of birth pains. Birth pains are the irreversible precursors of something new that will inevitably be birthed into existence. Truly, following these birth pains, something new that has never been before will be coming on the scene. In Section Two of this book, we will discuss in great detail what the birth pains are about and what it is that is being birthed.

And now, let us move on to the fifth of the seven signs that Jesus spoke of concerning the end of the age.

The Fifth Sign

Let us look closely at the Scriptures to see what happens after whatever it is that is being birthed is born. Matthew 24:9-21 describes what happens after the birth pains give way to the birth of something never seen before. Notice that the very first word of verse 9 is "Then," which denotes what follows the birth. Jesus said, "Then they will deliver you up to tribulation and kill you, and you will be hated by all nations for my name's sake." The Bible refers to these times of tribulation, persecution, and testing as a time of great tribulation such as has never been seen before or will ever be seen again. Take a look at this verse:

> **21For then there will be great tribulation, such as has not been since the beginning of the world until this time, no, nor ever shall be.** —Matthew 24:21

Many scholars identify the recipients of this great tribulation as either being natural Israel or worldly sinners. They describe this tribulation as judgment for their unbelief and evil ways. Upon taking a closer look at this passage, however, we can clearly see this is not so. Israel, as a nation, missed the day of her visitation and rejected her Messiah. The people Jesus is instructing in this passage are those who have received Jesus as their Messiah, resulting in their being ostracized and persecuted for His name's sake. Natural Jews and sinners will not choose to suffer for the sake of Jesus or His name. This passage sounds similar to the Luke 21 account of the tribulation that Jewish Christians suffered shortly after Christ's ascension and before the destruction of Jerusalem and the temple. However, this time it will be about all believers, not just Jewish believers. The Jewish believers in Luke 21 were the typological prophetic fulfillment. The last days believers are the ultimate prophetic fulfillment. Though these are not all Jews, they are referred to as being part of the "Jerusalem which is above" of whom all true believers are born.

> ²⁴...which things are symbolic. For these are the two covenants: the one from Mount Sinai which gives birth to bondage, which is Hagar– ²⁵for this Hagar is Mount Sinai in Arabia, and corresponds to Jerusalem which now is, and is in bondage with her children– ²⁶but the Jerusalem above is free, which is the mother of us all.
> —Galatians 4:24-26

Many Bible translations use the word "affliction" instead of "tribulation" in Matthew 24:9. However the Greek word, *thlipsis* which is translated as "affliction" in verse 9 of many translations is the same Greek word used and translated as "tribulation" in Matthew 24:21,29. It is clear that which immediately follows the birth pains and the birth in Matthew 24:8 is the great tribulation period. The Bible declares that it will be of greater magnitude than at any other time in the history of this age. As a matter of fact, this passage states that there shall never be tribulation of this magnitude in the future either. It is more than the world simply opposing us; we will be hated, not just disliked. There are Christians right now in Iran and China, as well as other countries, who are already experiencing a period of tribulation. How can it get any greater or worse than being imprisoned and/or slaughtered for His name's sake? There are pastors who have been executed in Iran because they will not renounce or deny Jesus Christ as their Lord and Savior. They would rather die for His name's sake than to deny Him. How can the conditions of the tribulation period be any worse than that? The difference is the universal scope of tribulation, which indeed makes it the greatest tribulation period of this age. It is great tribulation not because of the harshness of the treatment but the scope of the treatment. He is not addressing this teaching to a few disciples or a few countries. His target audience, in this passage of Scripture, is the entire Christian faith. All those who know or say that they believe in Jesus Christ will be hated. Why? They will be hated for His name's sake.

Many of those being tribulated will be overthrown in the wilderness testing even as was the case with natural Israel in her wilderness testing. This is clearly born out in Israel's biblical history, which can be seen in Hebrews 3. God said He was not well-pleased with many of them because they were overthrown in the wilderness. Some of us who are professing Christians today are being subjected to wilderness testings even before this time of great tribulation. God will not be pleased with us either if we are overthrown and overcome by the very test that He has purposed to prepare, build, and equip our lives. God has reserved the great tribulation for those who avoided or failed times of testing previously. It will be a time and means for Christians in the last days to be thoroughly purged and made ready as overcomers.

> [9]After these things I looked, and behold, a great multitude which no one could number, of all nations, tribes, peoples, and tongues, standing before the throne and before the Lamb, clothed with white robes, with palm branches in their hands, [10]and crying out with a loud voice, saying, "Salvation belongs to our God who sits on the throne, and to the Lamb!" [11]All the angels stood around the throne and the elders and the four living

creatures, and fell on their faces before the throne and worshiped God, [12]saying: "Amen! Blessing and glory and wisdom, thanksgiving and honor and power and might, be to our God forever and ever. Amen." [13]Then one of the elders answered, saying to me, "Who are these arrayed in white robes, and where did they come from?" [14]And I said to him, "Sir, you know." So he said to me, "These are the ones who come out of the great tribulation, and washed their robes and made them white in the blood of the Lamb."   —Revelation 7:9-14

The world system under the direct influence of the devil and his demons will be out to eradicate the church, which Satan knows is God's instrument of choice to usher in God's kingdom on this earth. The beast, the one-world government of the last days, will declare war on the church universal no matter what the denomination or affiliation. Both nominal Christians and genuine Christians alike will be cast into the great tribulation. Though the one-world system will not be able to discern between the true and false, God will. He will use this time of severe wilderness testing to separate the false from the true, the goats from the sheep. That which undergoes tribulation will respond in one of two ways – confessing the lordship of Jesus Christ for His name's sake or denying it. How will these happen?

Matthew 24:10 clearly speaks to this question. The means God will use to separate the true church from the false church is by their response to the very tribulation into which they are cast. Some will by faith endure the tribulation and many others will be offended. They will be overthrown and forsake the Lord and also forsake those who are truly His. The offended will align themselves with and pledge allegiance to the one-world empire to escape the persecution being imposed upon them. In so doing, they make themselves the enemies of the cross of Christ and partners with those who are the enemies of Christ and His true church. This makes them partners with and every bit as antichrist as the very Antichrist himself. The Greek word for *offended* in Matthew 24:10 is "skandalidzo" which means "to be scandalized, entrapped, enticed to sin, to fall into apostasy, or to fall into the displeasure of the Lord." This leads to the betrayal of the offended ones' natural and spiritual families. Betrayal such as this should never be found in the church, which is to be God's "holy place." And how will many be persuaded to switch their allegiance? It will be because of fear, their lack of spiritual discernment, and their lack of sound judgment caused by allowing their love for the Lord to grow cold. They will succumb to deception and be overthrown by the many false prophets who will come with signs and wonders following their ministries. Only those who endure to the end of these testings, commonly referred to as the great tribulation period, will be saved. I believe the love of many growing cold, generally speaking, is emblematic of the Laodicean age of the dispensation of the New Testament church. The letters written to the seven churches in Revelation chapters 2 and 3 were representative of the current conditions and states of these churches in 95 AD. I believe the Scriptures were typologically fulfilled with these seven literal churches. However, I believe the Scriptures represent a more prophetic fulfillment by the depiction of the various stages of the church from its inception to the end of the age. I also believe that during every stage or phase there were some who were better represented by one of the other seven church descriptions. For example, even though generally speaking the church today is best represented by the letter to Laodicea, there are some Christians such as in Iran and

China that would be better represented by the letter to Smyrna. Smyrna was a church in the midst of severe tribulation and persecution. Though some Christians may be better represented by one of the other six phases from Ephesus to Philadelphia, generally speaking most will be in the Laodicean spiritual state in the last days. They will be totally oblivious to their spiritual poverty. They will think that they are rich when they are really poor. They will think that they are hot when they are really cold. This makes them lukewarm in the eyes of the Lord. Even in this state, the Lord is faithful to knock at the door of their hearts, promising to come in if only they will open up to Him.

For those who recognize their spiritual poverty and have followed God's counsel to buy gold, white raiment, and eye salve, the Lord will help them greatly to endure this time of severe testing and great tribulation. The prevailing hardships that will cause many to deny Him will also cause some to be a witness for the Lord. This will result in an effectual preaching of the gospel into all the world by both their faithful words and their faithful actions. For many, the cost will be their very lives; they will be martyred. After the gospel has been effectively preached and demonstrated, then the end of the age will begin to approach rapidly, like a row of dominoes falling one right after another.

The life and death of Jesus serves as a model of spreading the gospel of the Kingdom in such a manner. Consider the day He died. How did He preach the gospel that day? Apparently His life and actions were enough to convince the thief on the cross next to Him that He was real. The thief, without any Bible teaching from Jesus, understood that Jesus was a King and that today He was going to return to His kingdom. Jesus' life and actions were such a witness of the good news of the gospel of the Kingdom that the thief was inspired to ask Jesus, "Be merciful to me, a sinner, and remember me when You come into Your Kingdom." So effective was Jesus' preaching of the gospel that day that a vile sinner was converted and received eternal life. Jesus confirmed his conversion by saying, "Today you will be with Me in paradise."

I am not inferring that you have to die to be a witness. The Greek word for "witness," however, is *martys* from which we get the word "martyr." You can be a witness of the gospel of the Kingdom without dying naturally but by dying to your own self-interests to serve life to others. These are they of whom it is written, "They loved not their lives even unto death." These are they who overcame by the blood of the Lamb and the word of their testimony.

Those who overcome understand that God is in control and that He is the Sovereign Potentate. They understand that the devil has no authority or ability to displace God's predetermined plan for their lives and that God's sovereignty is not in the least bit challenged by or subject to what the devil is attempting to do in their lives. As a matter of fact, they believe that the devil is subject to what God is doing in their lives through the faith and trust they place in the Almighty God.

We too, of this last generation, are challenged to be overcomers even in the midst of severe testing. We are able to do this by our right appropriation of the blood of the Lamb and the word of our testimony. God promises His children that if we truly believe, He will never put us into a test that is greater than what we are able to stand or bear, but will with the temptation provide us a way of escape, that we may be able to bear it.

[13]No temptation has overtaken you except such as is common to man; but God is faithful, who will not allow you

to be tempted beyond what you are able, but with the
temptation will also make the way of escape, that you
may be able to bear it.   —1 Corinthians 10:13

The issue is not whether we have trials and tests; the issue is
how are we going to respond when they come. We must understand that God has purposed tribulation not for the "ain'ts" but for
the "saints." There is something about tribulation that makes you
press harder into the kingdom of God. It teaches you something
of great value. There is a vital lesson to be learned. That's why Paul
said to the churches, you "must through much tribulation enter
into the kingdom of God (Acts 14:22 KJV). It is the reason why
Paul also said in Romans 5:3-5 that he gloried in tribulations. He
would never glory and value punishment or judgment. Tribulation offers a positive hope and outcome; judgment does not!

Some teachers say that God would never cast any of His children that He so dearly loves into tribulation. This is totally contrary to the Scriptures. Throughout the ages of God dealing with
His people, He has never been hesitant to lead His children into
the wilderness to be tested or tribulated. He has often chosen the
furnace of affliction for His children. We must understand that
the purpose of the tribulation period is to be a time of testing
and preparation, not a time of judgment. We will talk about the
time of judgment that God has reserved for the unbelievers of this
world in Section Two of this book. It is referred to as the great day
of God's wrath.

6

The Abomination of Desolation

The Abomination of Desolation

Now we want to continue talking about the tribulation of the saints and in particular, the abomination of desolation. It is described in Matthew 24:15 and Mark 13:14:

> [15]"Therefore when you see the 'abomination of desolation,' spoken of by Daniel the prophet, standing in the holy place" (whoever reads, let him understand)...
> —Matthew 24:15

> [14]"So when you see the 'abomination of desolation,' spoken of by Daniel the prophet, standing where it ought not" (let the reader understand), "then let those who are in Judea flee to the mountains." —Mark 13:14

Throughout the ages there have been many schools of thought as to what this abomination is in reference to leaving us, with a number of viewpoints to consider. Let me state at the outset, I personally do not believe it will be the Antichrist sacrificing a pig on the altar of a newly erected temple in Jerusalem. Such an event would not have a global or universal impact on all the people of the world. Remember, the apostles taught the believers that the temple in the New Testament is the church made without hands, not a temple erected through man's handiwork. Many Christians believe that a literal, physical temple must be constructed before the end of this age in which the abomination of desolation can take place. Though I believe that a temple will be constructed in the millennial kingdom, it is a difficult task to prove from the Scriptures that it will happen before the end of this age. Even if the Jews did rebuild the temple, why would God inhabit it? Why would God ever move back into a temple made with hands when that type of temple was merely to serve as a type and shadow of something greater to which God was pointing? The culmination that the shadow was pointing to was a temple made of living stones that God, Himself, would build and inhabit.

We must remember that God chose the descriptors by which this event is named. Whatever this is in reference to, we know from its very name that it is considered an abomination to God, and that it would cause desolation in the Holy Place. Without being dogmatic, I would like to offer another possible perspective concerning the abomination of desolation that seems to flow naturally out of the context of the Scriptures that precede its description.

Abomination and Desolation – Who and Where?

First of all, God described it as an abomination. The Greek word for abomination is *bdelugma* and it means "a foul or detestable thing." There are many Scriptures in which God describes what is an abomination to Him. One of the most notable of those Scriptures is found in Proverbs 6:16-19.

> [16]These six things the Lord hates, yes, seven are an abomination to Him: [17]A proud look, a lying tongue, hands that shed innocent blood, [18]a heart that devises wicked plans, feet that are swift in running to evil, [19]a false witness who speaks lies, and one who sows discord among brethren.   —Proverbs 6:16-19

When you take the seventh offense and use it as the context for the previous six, it is clear that all seven things are to God an abomination. All these things God detests because they have to do with violations against, and betrayal of, relationships. All sin, whether against God or man, is a violation of relationship. A quick look at the Ten Commandments confirms that this is so. For example, to have any other god is a violation of your relationship with God; to not honor your parents is a violation of a relationship; to steal from your neighbor is a violation of a relationship, etc.

In reading the accounts in Matthew and Mark that precede the description of the abomination of desolation, we see the context is the betrayal of covenantal relationships by the many who are offended as a result of having been delivered up to tribulation. The account in Mark is the most graphic and detailed description of that which will take place.

> [12]Now brother will betray brother to death, and a father his child; and children will rise up against parents and cause them to be put to death.   —Mark 13:12

Imagine how much of an abomination it must be to God that brother will betray brother, the father the son, and children against the parents, causing their deaths. Though these things have happened throughout the history of mankind, the thing that makes it such an abomination to God is where it happens. The Mark 13 account says that this abomination happens where it ought never to happen. It happens in the Holy Place, which is inside the temple of God, according to the Matthew 24 account. We know from the Scriptures that the church is the temple of God or God's house on this earth. God says that those affected by the desolation are those who confess the name of Jesus and His lordship. As we have said earlier, the people being tribulated and persecuted even unto death are the saints of God. It is clear that the ones that cause these saints to be turned over to the worldly authorities would be those who claim to have a relationship with the Lord and with those they betray. I believe many of these will be professing Christians who are Christians in name only. When they are cast into tribulation and are persecuted, these will deny Christ, their natural family, and their spiritual family. These profess to be believers of Christ, and many will be members of local churches.

This betrayal and this discord amongst the brethren is an abomination and it causes desolation in the house of God. First Corinthians 3:16-17 serves as a sober warning when it asks the question, "Do you not know that you [2nd person plural] are the temple of God and that the Spirit of God dwells in you?" This Scripture goes on to say that if any man defiles this temple, God will destroy him. This is the plight of all those who are overthrown in this time of tribulation.

We know these things will happen because they are prophetically declared by God, but woe unto those who bring the offense. Church history confirms that after the ascension of Jesus the Jewish believers of the church in Jerusalem were beaten, imprisoned, and even executed for their faith in Jesus. I believe that which happened in the beginning days of the church serves as a shadow and hint as to what will happen in the last days of the church. Israel's history is a typological pattern for the end of the age.

> ¹¹Now all these things happened to them as examples, and they were written for our admonition, upon whom the ends of the ages have come.   —1 Corinthians 10:11

The devil's purpose in all of this is to destroy the church, but God's purpose is to purge, purify, and strengthen His church.

Counsel During the Abomination of Desolation

Whether or not the abomination of desolation is the betrayal of both natural and spiritual covenantal relationships is an issue that remains to be seen. However, the counsel of God to His people is clear; they are to flee when they see these things begin to happen.

Again we must understand that what happened to the Jewish Christians in Jerusalem at the beginning of the church age was typological in its fulfillment. The tribulation that was described in Luke 21 was to happen before all the other signs that were to mark the end of the age. Its impact was localized. At the end of the church age, however, I believe the church that is tribulated is from every nation, kindred, and tongue. I believe this tribulation, like all the other signs, are global in their impact. Therefore I believe the instructions in the Matthew account are addressed to all those who profess to be Christians throughout the whole world. Even the terms that seem to be local are just symbolic of a more literal, universal instruction. Judea represented the area surrounding

Jerusalem, which was the central focus or center of living of the early church. Judea in the literal last days' fulfillment, I believe, represents the area that touches the boundaries of our central life and focus. During the time of the great tribulation, I believe it will be important that Christians abandon their normal course of life. The unified world will be seeking to identify who these radical believers are. The first place they might look for these would be in the advertised services of their local churches. I believe the church will follow the example of today's persecuted church by becoming the last days' universal underground church.

Consider that the first word in Matthew 24:15 is "Therefore." "Therefore" is there to say that based on the context of the verses preceding verse 15, here is specific instruction or counsel as to how we should posture ourselves during these events. Jesus said that when you see the abomination that makes desolate, "Flee!" Why? Matthew 24:21 answers that question. It says that when you see the betrayal of relationships and the abomination of desolation, THEN shall follow great tribulation such as has never been before or will ever be again. According to Matthew 24:22, so great will be that tribulation that if the Lord did not shorten those days, no flesh would be saved or spared. However, for the sake of His elect, Jesus will shorten those days.

When these things come to pass, God's wise counsel is to be on guard for false christs (ministers with false anointings) and false prophets who will show great signs and wonders to deceive the multitudes. The next several verses in Matthew 24 make clear that when Christ comes, no one will have to tell anyone that He is here or there. Every eye will see Him in the day of His vengeance, whether kings or paupers, great or small. It says that His coming will be like the lightning that shines from the East and flashes to the West; all will see it and know who He is. How far can you see a big lightning bolt that flashes across the sky? It can be miles away and still be clearly and easily seen.

Being an instrument-rated pilot, I can tell you from experience that lightning bolts can be seen from greater distances than one might imagine. I remember one night I was flying our six-passenger plane from Ohio to minister in Wisconsin. The weather was very rainy and we were on an IFR flight plan. My wife and I couldn't see anything until we finally broke out on top of the clouds on that dark rainy night some 350 miles from our point of departure. Off in the distance ahead of us, I could see lightning flashes. With still being 100 miles out from our final destination, it appeared that we would hit a thunderstorm before we arrived there. I began to look at my charts for another airport to land at within the next thirty miles. I just kept flying and was amazed that we still hadn't gotten to the point of where the lightning was. We landed at our final destination and I could still see the lightning on the horizon in front of us. That which looked to be 20 or 30 miles ahead of us turned out to be more like 150 miles in front of us.

In the next chapter of this book we will discuss what happens after the great tribulation when Jesus comes, and what will be the signs of His coming.

7

Post-Tribulation Events: Signs 6 & 7

Things to Remember

Jesus began to teach about some major prophetic events and happenings that would take place in the last days. We know that what Jesus taught from this earth will not contradict what He taught from heaven concerning eschatology or any other subject.

It is also important to remember to whom Jesus' eschatological teaching was given. We have already discussed in previous chapters of this book that the target audience to whom God was speaking of these end time events was spiritual Israel (not natural Israel), those of Israel who had been born from above. These were the disciples that followed Him. He actually taught them these things in a private conversation. Those disciples were the very firstfruits of the New Testament church. They were born of the spirit of God; their names were written in the Lamb's Book of Life. Jesus wanted His people to know what the future held for them. Why? So they would not be taken by surprise when these prophecies began to come to pass in real time.

The three gospel accounts of the Olivet Discourse warn of a time of tribulation. The *literal typological prophetic fulfillment* has already happened; it is found in the Luke 21 passage. This tribulation happened to the believing Jews shortly after His ascension even to the time of the destruction of Jerusalem in 70 AD. The believers in the very last days will experience the *literal ultimate prophetic fulfillment*. For both groups, it was and will be great tribulation the likes of which they had never experienced before. For the end time believers, this tribulation will be the greatest that will ever be, not because of the severity of what happens but because of the universal magnitude of what will happen. What can be more severe than being martyred for your faith? Death is death. This is what happened to many of God's people in the early church. This typological fulfillment was isolated to a very small geographical area and a relatively small number of people. However, in the last days the tribulation will be of a much greater scale. It will be a time when many believers of all kindreds, nations, and tongues will be tribulated. Its scope will be worldwide, not just in the Middle East as before. As it was with the typological fulfillment, so shall it be with the ultimate fulfillment in the last days. All will be persecuted; many will be martyred; some will survive.

People need to be warned about what lies ahead in the last days. As a matter of fact, one of the purposes of the anointing was to do this very thing.

> [1]"The Spirit of the Lord God *is* upon Me, because the Lord has anointed Me to preach good tidings to the poor; He has sent Me to heal the brokenhearted, to proclaim

liberty to the captives, and the opening of the prison to
those who are bound; ²To proclaim the acceptable year of
the Lord, and the day of vengeance of our God."
—Isaiah 61:1-2

From this Scripture we can see that one of the purposes of the
anointing is to proclaim the acceptable year of the Lord and the
day of vengeance of our God. The word *proclaim* means "to cry
out, to summon through an invitation." We're supposed to cry out
loud and proclaim something. What are we to proclaim? We are to
proclaim two things in addition to the preaching of the gospel. We
need to declare to the world and the church about the acceptable
year of the Lord and the day of the vengeance of our God. I believe
the acceptable year of the Lord is speaking about none other than
the Year of Jubilee. In the history of Israel, every 50 years was to
be the Year of Jubilee. It followed the year after seven consecutive "Shemitahs," each of which occurred every seven years. Every
seventh year was to be a year of rest in which the land was not to
be planted or harvested. It was also a year in which all debts were
cancelled. If you owed a debt you couldn't pay, you had to work it
off to that person; you became a servant or a slave to that person.
Some people even had to go to debtor's prison. However, every
50 years, during the Year of Jubilee, the Lord's command was that
all property and possessions be returned to the original owners.
This was in addition to the release of debts forgiven in the previous year, which would have been the seventh year of the seventh
consecutive Shemitah.

Concerning the day of the vengeance of our God, we will
cover that topic in this next subtopic.

Post-Tribulation Events

And now let us begin to look at what will take place in the last generation after the great tribulation.

The Sixth Sign

Matthew 24:29 says that immediately following the tribulation of those days described in the preceding verses, there would be very dramatic events taking place.

> [29]"Immediately after the tribulation of those days the sun will be darkened, and the moon will not give its light; the stars will fall from heaven, and the powers of the heavens will be shaken."   —Matthew 24:29

One has to wonder what these cataclysmic happenings are going to be like when they are actually experienced by men. These events affect the earth, the heavens, and even the powers and principalities of the spiritual realm. The Luke account is very graphic about the unfolding of these events. There will be so much distress and perplexity in the nations that men's hearts will actually fail them from fear of what is going to happen next! Even the powers and principalities in heavenly places will be shaken to their very core.

> [25]"And there will be signs in the sun, in the moon, and in the stars; and on the earth distress of nations, with perplexity, the sea and the waves roaring; [26]men's hearts failing them from fear and the expectation of those things which are coming on the earth, for the powers of the heavens will be shaken.   —Luke 21:25-26

Matthew 24:30 says that immediately following these cata-clysmic events, the coming of Jesus would be witnessed by all who inhabit the earth. Believe me when I say that God will not need to depend on modern technologies such as TV or the Internet to cause all who are on this earth to see Him. This revelation of Him will be supernatural, not natural. Every eye will see Him whether they are watching TV or on the Internet, or not.

> ³⁰Then the sign of the Son of Man will appear in heaven, and then <u>all the tribes of the earth will mourn</u>, and <u>they will see the Son of Man coming</u> on the clouds of heaven with power and great glory.   —Matthew 24:30

The Seventh Sign

Matthew 24:31 says that after all who are on the earth see the Son of Man coming with power and great glory, the angels will gather the elect of God from the entire earth. This happens after the sixth sign but before He commences the fearful judgments of the seventh sign upon all those who dwell on the earth.

> ³¹And He will send His angels with a great sound of a trumpet, and they will gather together His elect from the four winds, from one end of heaven to the other.
> —Matthew 24:31

These two signs that happen immediately after the great tribu-lation are not indicative of the second coming of the Lord. Most readers just assume that any passage of Scripture that talks about the coming of the Lord or the day of the Lord has to do with the second coming of the Lord to this earth.

When we see these things unfolding, we must ask ourselves which "coming of the Lord" is being referred to – the day of His vengeance or the acceptable year of the Lord? How can we know? We can know by the events that are unfolding and by who is being gathered first, the elect or the sinners. There are Scriptures that depict both scenarios concerning the reaping order. In one place He says He is going to gather first the elect. In another place, He talks about gathering together first the tares or sinners. The reason for this apparent biblical contradiction revolves around the fact that He is talking about two different events or comings, which are going to happen at two different times.

I want to talk about these two comings of the Lord because of the lack of realization of some that there is the day of the Lord's vengeance and the day of the Lord's return. These are two very different events. These are often confused as being one, and yet they are distinctly different in purpose and appearance. They are not to be viewed as being synonymous. No one will ever have to tell you when the day of the Lord comes. If someone has to tell you, it hasn't happened yet. Jesus also warned His people that in those days false christs and false prophets will arise and will show great signs and wonders so that, if possible, even the elect would be deceived. That means that some of God's people are here on this earth during that time period, which takes place after the tribulation period.

Jesus told His people these things so that they would know ahead of time and wouldn't be caught off guard. I repeat that no one will have to tell you when the day of Lord comes. I believe there will be those who try to convince you that it has happened. We see that the Thessalonians cried out because they thought that the day of the Lord had come and they had missed something.

Paul had to tell them that it indeed hadn't happened yet. He reminded them of some things that had to happen first as signs prior to this event. I personally believe that the day of the Lord is closer than we might think. It will be obvious when it comes upon the sinners to punish them.

I have heard people say that they are looking forward to the day of the Lord. We need to understand what this day is all about. There's a difference between the judgment of sinners in the day of the Lord and the establishment of the millennial kingdom at His second coming. These are totally different events but Jesus is depicted as coming in both of them. The day of the Lord will happen near the end of the age and the second coming will happen at the very end of the age.

The context of the Olivet Discourse is not indicative of the return of the Lord but rather of the day of His vengeance. At this juncture I want to direct you to a passage of Scripture that is not found in any of the Olivet Discourse passages. However, it brings much clarity to this day we are supposed to be proclaiming by the anointing. It is found in Isaiah 13, which speaks of this same time frame about which we have been talking. This happens before the second coming. Look what it says in Isaiah 13:6-11.

> [6]Wail, for the day of the Lord is at hand; as destruction from the Almighty and Sufficient One [Shaddai] will it come! [7]Therefore will all hands be feeble, and every man's heart will melt. [8]And they [of Babylon] shall be dismayed and terrified, pangs and sorrows shall take hold of them; they shall be in pain as a woman in childbirth. They will gaze stupefied and aghast at one another, their faces will be aflame [from the effects of the unprecedented warfare]. [9]Behold, the day of the Lord is coming! – fierce,

with wrath and raging anger – to make the land and the
[whole] earth a desolation and to destroy out of it its
sinners. [10]For the stars of the heavens and their constellations will not give their light; the sun will be darkened
at its rising and the moon will not shed its light. [11]And I,
the Lord, will punish the world for its evil, and the wicked for their guilt and iniquity; I will cause the arrogance
of the proud to cease and will lay low the haughtiness of
the terrible and the boasting of the violent and ruthless.
                                              —Isaiah 13:6-11 AMPC

This is prophetic; this is going to happen whether we believe it
or not. God does not need our permission. He says the sun will be
darkened; the moon will not cause its light to shine. Isaiah 13:11
says that He will punish the world for its evil, and the wicked for
their iniquity. He will halt the arrogance of the proud, He will lay
low the pompous pride of the ruthless. God also says that He will
show wonders in the heavens above and signs in earth beneath,
blood and fire and vapor of smoke. The sun will be turned into
darkness and the moon into blood before the coming of the great
and awesome and terrible day of the Lord. We need to know
these things because we are to proclaim the day of His vengeance.
Remember God says, "Vengeance is Mine, I will repay," (Rom.
12:19). There is coming a day when the people of this world will
be called into account for all the evil and injustices committed
against God's people. These people may look like they're getting
their way and prospering now, but they are going to be absolutely
terrified by this time of great judgment. There will be no salvation
from that point on; they had their chance; it will be too late for
salvation when Jesus comes to punish the sinners. The voice of
the bride and the bridegroom will no longer be heard in that day.

Everybody is going to know who Jesus is in the day of the Lord. It is an event on God's prophetic calendar coming sooner than most Christians may think. We need to warn and prepare people for this coming of the Lord even as Noah did in his day before God came to judge the earth and her inhabitants.

Though we need to educate people as to what is going to happen, no one will have to be told when it does happen. Matthew 24:27 says that the coming of the Son of Man will be like the lightning that shines from the east to the west. In verse 28 Jesus quotes the ancient proverb, "Wherever the carcass is, there the eagles will be gathered together." Wherever wicked people are, there will be assembled the instruments of their chastisement. He says that the providence of God will direct them there as the vultures are directed to a dead carcass. Not only will evil people be there, but also the instruments of their chastisement and judgment will be drawn there alike. Matthew 24:30 says that then the sign of the Son of Man will appear in heaven and all the tribes of the earth shall mourn, for they shall see Him coming on the clouds of heaven with power and great glory.

What coming is He describing in Matthew 24:30? As was mentioned before, we can know what coming He is talking about by the nature of the events that are unfolding and by who is being reaped first – the tares or the wheat. Matthew 13 records seven parables concerning the kingdom of God. The disciples privately asked Jesus the interpretation of just the first two of the seven parables. The second parable was the parable of the wheat and tares found in Matthew 13:36-43.

[36]Then Jesus sent the multitude away and went into the house. And His disciples came to Him, saying, "Explain

to us the parable of the tares of the field." [37]He answered and said to them: "He who sows the good seed is the Son of Man. [38]The field is the world, the good seeds are the sons of the kingdom, but the tares are the sons of the wicked one. [39]The enemy who sowed them is the devil, the harvest is the end of the age, and the reapers are the angels. [40]Therefore as the tares are gathered and burned in the fire, so it will be at the end of this age. [41]The Son of Man will send out His angels, and they will gather out of His kingdom all things that offend, and those who practice lawlessness, [42]and will cast them into the furnace of fire. There will be wailing and gnashing of teeth. [43]Then the righteous will shine forth as the sun in the kingdom of their Father. He who has ears to hear, let him hear.   —Matthew 13:36-43

Notice in this parable, the reaping order has the tares (sinners) first, and it occurs at the end of the age. Matthew 13:40-44 links the happenings of this parable to describe more clearly what will occur at the end of this age. As the tares are gathered and burned in the fire, so it will be at the end of this age. He will gather together first the tares to be bound and cast into the fiery torments of hell through death. This particular punishment comes at the end of the age before the millennial kingdom is established. God is going to rid the earth of the influence of the wicked. Even the devil is going to be bound for that thousand years. The inhabitants of the world are going to live for a thousand years with Jesus as the King over the whole world and with we, His saints, ruling and reigning with Him. Before one can accurately determine which coming of the Lord is being referenced in a passage of Scripture, it must be discerned who is being gathered first, the elect or the tares? If the reaping order is the elect first, then it speaks of the coming of the great day of the Lord. However, if the tares are being reaped first, then it is speaking about the second coming of Jesus at the end of this age.

It is interesting to note that in the Matthew 24 passage, the wheat (the elect) are being reaped first. This can be seen in verse 31, where Jesus is talking about the terrible day of the Lord and says that He will send His angels with a great sound of a trumpet and they will gather together His elect from the four winds, from one end of heaven to the other. The notable thing here is that He is going to gather together the elect from the four corners of the earth before the terrible judgments of the Lord begin and this is going to happen after the great tribulation.

> [31] And He will send His angels with a great sound of a trumpet, and they will gather together His elect from the four winds, from one end of heaven to the other.
> —Matthew 24:31

This would indicate that this coming does not refer to His second coming at the end of the age, but rather His coming to execute the great day of the Lord's wrath just prior to the end of the age. This is the day of His vengeance, commonly referred to as the great day of the wrath of the Lamb. It is a time of great judgment on those wicked people on the earth who have sworn allegiance to the Antichrist and his one-world government, who persecuted God's people. During this judgment, I believe His elect will be kept much like the children of Israel were kept in the land of Goshen during the last seven plagues that came to judge Egypt. Later in our study of Matthew 24, we will substantiate that this very reaping order, the elect before the tares, is the context of the Olivet Discourse.

8

Jerusalem, Another Sign

Another Sign

Before we continue this study, I would like to point out another sign of which we should take note. This sign is prophesied to happen even before the time of the unfolding of the great tribulation. It is recorded in Luke 21 and it concerns the "times of the Gentiles."

> [24]And they will fall by the edge of the sword, and be led away captive into all nations. And Jerusalem will be trampled by Gentiles until the times of the Gentiles are fulfilled. [25]"And there will be signs in the sun, in the moon, and in the stars.   —Luke 21:24-25

It says that Jerusalem will be under the control of the Gentiles until the times of the Gentiles be fulfilled. This means that from 70 AD when the city of Jerusalem fell into the hands and the authority of the Gentiles until Israel regained control of the city, the "times of the Gentiles" were not yet fulfilled. The Gentiles lost control of Jerusalem in the Six-Day War of 1967. Then in

Luke 21:28, Jesus instructed the terminal generation of this age that when you see these things begin to happen, look up, your redemption draws near. Many who are living today have witnessed this end time event as it took place in real time.

Remember, there were three questions asked by Jesus' disciples, which constituted the basis of the Olivet Discourse teaching Jesus preached. In addressing the question concerning "The Sign of His Coming," Jesus began to teach an important principle to illustrate that God's people should be able to discern the signs of the spiritual seasons in which they are living. This principle can be seen in Matthew 16:1-3 and Luke 12:54-56, as well as in Matthew 24:32-35 of the Olivet Discourse.

> [1]Then the Pharisees and Sadducees came, and testing Him asked that He would show them a sign from heaven. [2]He answered and said to them, "When it is evening you say, 'It will be fair weather, for the sky is red'; [3]and in the morning, 'It will be foul weather today, for the sky is red and threatening.' Hypocrites! You know how to discern the face of the sky, but you cannot discern the signs of the times?   —Matthew 16:1-3

> [54]Then He also said to the multitudes, "Whenever you see a cloud rising out of the west, immediately you say, 'A shower is coming'; and so it is. [55]And when you see the south wind blow, you say, 'There will be hot weather'; and there is. [56]Hypocrites! You can discern the face of the sky and of the earth, but how is it you do not discern this time?   —Luke 12:54-56

From these verses, we can see that there is an expectation by God of all who have been made alive spiritually, through the new birth, to be able to discern spiritual things. When we were born naturally, God equipped us with our natural senses to fully relate to and discern the natural world into which we were born. The same is true of our spiritual birth. God equipped us with the spiritual eyes, spiritual ears, and other spiritual senses to fully relate to and discern the spiritual world of which we were also born. Jesus describes those who say that they have been born spiritually and cannot discern the signs of the times as hypocrites.

Even the simplest of people know when to take shelter because of a coming thunderstorm. They know what is coming by looking at the signs on the horizon. Very early in life people learn the principle that ominous, dark clouds building on the horizon are a sign of an approaching storm. Should those who exercise their spiritual senses be any less perceptive? Should they not be alerted to the approaching spiritual storms which will dramatically affect their natural life, so that they too might have time to prepare and take shelter?

The Parable of the Fig Tree

In all three Olivet Discourse passages, Jesus cited the parable of the fig tree to reinforce this very important principle.

> [29]Then He spoke to them a parable: "Look at the fig tree, and all the trees. [30]When they are already budding, you see and know for yourselves that summer is now near. [31]So you also, when you see these things happening, know that the kingdom of God is near. [32]Assuredly, I say to you, this generation will by no means pass away till all things take place. [33]Heaven and earth will pass away, but My words will by no means pass away. —Luke 21:29-33

He says that we should learn from this parable of the fig tree. When its branches start budding and bringing forth leaves, we know that summer is near. This knowledge comes from observing what is happening with our natural senses. In the same way, we need to observe what is happening with our spiritual senses. He exhorts us that when we see the signs described in the previous verses happening, we ought to know that the coming of Lord is near. In Luke 21, He says that when we see these end time signs *begin* to happen, we are to look up because our redemption draws near. These signs have already begun to happen.

> **28Now when these things begin to happen, look up and lift up your heads, because your redemption draws near." 29Then He spoke to them a parable: "Look at the fig tree, and all the trees. 30When they are already budding, you see and know for yourselves that summer is now near. 31So you also, when you see these things happening, know that the kingdom of God is near. 32Assuredly, I say to you, this generation will by no means pass away till all things take place. 33Heaven and earth will pass away, but My words will by no means pass away. —Luke 21:28-33**

Jesus goes on to say in this parable that the generation that sees these signs begin to happen will not pass away until all things take place. He indicates that heaven and earth have a better chance of passing away than this terminal generation.

This begs the question, "What is considered to be a generation?" This is only my opinion, but I believe that approximately every twenty years a new generation begins to be birthed. Let me share with you why I believe this is true. God seemed to make that same distinction in Israel when He said that all those who were twenty years old and above were accountable to give offerings to the Lord and if able-bodied they were to go to war. When judging Israel for their disobedience in the wilderness, it seemed to be God's cutoff point or age of accountability as to who would be allowed to enter the promised land or not.

Keep in mind that there are usually four generations living at the same time. Occasionally you might see a five-generation family picture. Normally, there is the young generation (up to 20 years old), the producing (fathers and mothers) generation of 20-40 years old, the grandparent generation of 40-60 years old, and the great grandparent generation of 60-80 years old. I believe the current or active generation of any time period is the producing generation. The other three generations are either those who are yet to produce or those who have already produced in another generation, season or time period. The Bible seems to support this notion in a number of Scriptures that talk about the fourth (or four) generations. One such passage is found in Exodus 34:7 where God says that He will visit the iniquity of the fathers upon the children and the children's children even to the third and the fourth generation. In 2 Kings 10:30, God told Jehu that because he did well, his sons would sit on the throne of Israel to the fourth generation.

Earlier in this chapter, we discussed the sign of the "times of the Gentiles." The active or producing generation that saw Jerusalem restored to Israel in 1967 were those who were 20-40 years old at the time. Could it be that this is the terminal generation as well as all the generations that are younger? Could it be that this is the generation being referred to in the parable of the fig tree as the one that will not pass away until all things be fulfilled?

Joel 2:28-3:2 indicates that the generation that sees Israel restored to her land and Jerusalem restored to Israel would also in that same day or same time period see the sun darkened, the moon turned to blood, the coming of the day of the Lord, the outpouring of the Holy Spirit, and the battle of Armageddon. If we truly believe that we are a part of the last or terminal generation, these things are especially applicable to us. We then are the very generation Jesus was speaking to when He said, "Look up ... your redemption draws near" (Luke 21:28).

9

Look Up and Watch

What Does "Looking Up" Entail?

What does Luke 21:28 mean where it says that we are to look up and lift up our heads?

> ²⁸**Now when these things begin to happen, look up and lift up your heads, because your redemption draws near.**
> —**Luke 21:28**

In the Greek, the word for "look up" means to stop bending down or to lift one's body and/or soul because of elation; the word for "lift up your heads" means to poise one's self by lifting up one's head because of what is coming.

If you can tell when a harvest is due by ripe fruit, you can tell when a spiritual event is going to happen also. Jesus tells them that, as is the case with the fig tree, so it is that you can know when prophetic events are about to happen by looking at the biblical signs associated with them. The Bible declares that no one except the Father in heaven knows the day or the hour of this coming. However, God does not say that we cannot know the year or the month or the season. The Scriptures portray God's people as sons of light. He expects us to, at the very least, know the spiritual season in which we are living. Therefore, His children need to be watching for these signs so that the day of the Lord might not take them by surprise.

The Luke 21 account gives even more specific definition and instruction regarding this exhortation of the Lord.

> [34]"But take heed to yourselves, lest your hearts be weighed down with carousing, drunkenness, and cares of this life, and that Day come on you unexpectedly. [35]For it will come as a snare on all those who dwell on the face of the whole earth. [36]Watch therefore, and pray always that you may be counted worthy to escape all these things that will come to pass, and to stand before the Son of Man."
> —Luke 21:34-36

The first thing Jesus teaches concerning that to which we must give our attention is our daily lifestyle. So many Christians are spiritually asleep and caught up in the pleasures of this life. They are weighed down with carousings, drunkenness, and the cares of this life. Paul warned Timothy about these very dangers in the last days.

> [1]But know this, that in the last days perilous times will come: [2]For men will be lovers of themselves, lovers of money, boasters, proud, blasphemers, disobedient to parents, unthankful, unholy, [3]unloving, unforgiving, slanderers, without self-control, brutal, despisers of good, [4]traitors, headstrong, haughty, lovers of pleasure rather than lovers of God, [5]having a form of godliness but denying its power. And from such people turn away.
> —2 Timothy 3:1-5

The second thing Jesus teaches concerning that to which we must give our attention is that of watching and praying. Why is it important that we watch and pray? Jesus says this will be the very criteria by which we will be counted worthy or deserving of escaping all the aforementioned adversities. If we watch and pray, we will not be surprised by the day of the Lord which is coming expressly to punish sinners on the whole earth.

Learning from Types and Shadows

Jesus often referenced historical types and shadows to bring greater clarity to that which He was teaching. This is the case in two of the Olivet Discourse passages, as He was teaching about the signs that would precede the coming of the day of the vengeance of our God. The historical type and shadow Jesus used to describe the days preceding the day of the Lord was the days of Noah.

> [37]But as the days of Noah were, so also will the coming of the Son of Man be. [38]For as in the days before the flood, they were eating and drinking, marrying and giving in marriage, until the day that Noah entered the ark, [39]and did not know until the flood came and took them all away, so also will the coming of the Son of Man be.
>
> —Matthew 24:37-39

He says that the coming of the Son of Man will be just like it was in the days of Noah. Most people assume that this coming is in reference to Christ's second coming or the return of the Lord to set up His kingdom. I would beg to differ with this assumption. I believe that this coming is in reference to the day of the Lord or, as I previously stated, the day of the vengeance of our God. I believe this can be substantiated in this same passage of Scripture by the very verses that follow His assertion.

As in the days before the flood, they were eating and drinking, marrying and giving in marriage, until the day Noah entered the ark. They were carrying on with life as usual. Their mindset was that normal life was going to continue as it had been, indefinitely. They didn't realize until it was too late that this was not the fact. It was not too late until Noah and his family entered the ark and God sealed the door. He sealed Noah and his family so that they would not be affected by the judgment that was about to take place all around them.

If you are an overcoming Christian who is alive at the time of the day of the Lord, it is important for you to know that God has not appointed you to wrath. If you are truly one of His, He will seal you so you will not be affected by the impending judgment and punishment that is coming. He says that in Noah's day they didn't realize judgment was coming until the flood came and took them away. This same blindness and obliviousness will be the case once again at the time of the coming of the Son of Man in the day of the Lord.

Jesus further describes the fate of those taken in judgment in the next two verses of this passage.

> **40Then two men will be in the field: one will be taken and the other left. 41Two women will be grinding at the mill: one will be taken and the other left.**
> **—Matthew 24:40-41**

These verses say that then two men will be in the field – one will be taken, the other left; two women will be grinding at the mill – one will be taken and the other left. The mistake that many make when interpreting this passage is that they assume that the word "took" in Matthew 24:39 is the same word for "taken" in Matthew 24:40-41. However, that is not the case. In verse 39, the word "took" refers to those taken in judgment by the flood. The word for "took" in that verse is the Greek word *Iro*. This word means to remove, to take away what is another's by force, to take from among the living either by natural death or by violence. This definition fits with the *literal typological prophetic fulfillment* of Noah's day. The flood came and punished them and took them away by violence. Likewise, it will be indicative of the *literal ultimate prophetic fulfillment* in the day of the Lord. He is going to come and cause them to be taken in judgment after He has finished sealing His people from the coming wrath.

Now let us take a closer look at the Greek words used in Matthew 24:40-41. The Greek words for "taken" and "left" found in both verses are the same. The Greek word for "taken" is not *Iro* as in Matthew 24:39. It is *paralambano*. The definition of this word is very interesting. It means to join with oneself, to associate with as a companion, to take near to oneself. Does that sound like a person taken in judgment? No, that's the one that Jesus is going to take to Himself to protect and shelter. It says, one will be taken and the other left. The Greek word for "left" is *aphiemi*. The definition of this word is also very interesting and revealing. It means to send away, to depart from as a husband divorcing his wife, to let go of, to leave so that what is left will remain, or to abandon and leave destitute. It is evident from this that in the case of the two men and two women, one will be taken to be a companion with Jesus, and the other will be left as in a divorce to be destroyed.

The Reaping Order Revisited

Earlier, in chapter seven of this book, we discussed how we could determine which coming of the Lord is being referenced in a passage of Scripture. The way we can know what *coming* God is talking about is by the nature of the related events that are unfolding and by who is being reaped first ... the tares or the wheat.

As it was in the days of Noah, so shall it be in the days of the coming of the Son of Man. God will gather His people first and seal them. Afterwards, He shall gather the wicked in all the earth to punish them. In this case God is reaping the wheat before the tares. The reaping order of Matthew 24:39-41 reaffirms that the context of the Olivet Discourse is speaking about the day of the Lord near the end of the age and not the return of the Lord at the very end of the age.

Not only are we supposed to know about both of these prophetic events, but also we are supposed to teach and proclaim these by the anointing. Do you know what Noah did in the daytime? He built an ark. Do you know what he did at night? He went and preached to the very people who were mocking his ministry; he was called the preacher of righteousness. He was anointed to go and preach the gospel to the world and warn them of the day of judgment that would surely come to pass in their lifetime. Noah was anointed to preach and warn; Jesus was anointed to preach and warn. Why do you think God's people have received the anointing in these last days? Surely it is to preach the gospel of deliverance and healing to those in need and to proclaim the day of the Lord's vengeance and the acceptable year of the Lord.

It is time for us to be sober and about our Father's business. It is time for us to allow the anointing to flow through us for the purpose for which He was given. And this we are to do no matter what the response of the people might be. We were not anointed to please man but to please God. The Bible says that if we seek to please man, we cannot be the servants of Christ. Ministering under the anointing does not guarantee acceptance, approval, and appreciation by the people to whom we minister. Just look at the examples of Jesus and Noah.

In Section Two of this book, we will be looking at what Jesus taught concerning eschatology from heaven through the apostles and prophets. As we begin the study of what He taught from heaven, we know that one thing is sure. What He taught the apostles and prophets from heaven will be in total agreement with what He taught His disciples while He was with them on this earth. I know I have shared this principle several times already in this book, but I feel it bears repeating again and again, that it might truly resonate in our spirits.

Never again lose sight of the fact that these things are going to happen. They are already beginning to unfold. May the Lord help us to watch unto prayer, that we would not be overtaken by the cares and issues of this life. Let us not be like those who mortgage their future to satisfy the desires of their present yearnings.

Section Two:

What Jesus Taught on Eschatology from Heaven

10

Intro to the Book
of Revelation

Introduction

As we continue our study, let us not lose sight of the fact that the responsibility to be a Berean (see Acts 17:10-11) is that of the reader and not the writer. As a student of the Word of God, it should be more important for you to be willing to move to truth than it is to prove the position you currently embrace to be right. In settling issues of doctrine, do not force the Scriptures to walk your talk or doctrinal position; let the Scriptures talk to determine your walk or doctrinal position. When our position satisfies one Scripture yet violates another, we must look to be enlightened to a position that satisfies both.

We must always remember that the revelatory teachings of Jesus from heaven will never contradict or change what He taught on the earth. Any interpretation from the prophetic books of the Bible must be in full agreement with and congruent to Christ's teachings in the Olivet Discourse. With this in mind, let us begin Section Two.

Our Focus

Whereas in Section One we focused on what Jesus taught about end time events while He was on the earth, in Section Two our focus will be on what Jesus taught about eschatology from heaven through revelation to His servants, the apostles and prophets.

It is my prayer that our study of eschatology would not be as informational as it would be revelational; that it would not be as educational as it would be motivational. For this to happen, we must understand that preconceived ideas and theologies can be a hindrance. We must be willing to verify all of our embraced theologies from the Word of God, or dispose of them. We need to be leery of dogmatism on eschatology and of those who seem to have it "ALL" figured out. I will try to separate for the reader those things that I feel I have received by revelation from those things that represent my personal opinion. I will try to preface the latter with phrases such as "I believe," or "I personally believe," or "It is my opinion," or "I feel," or "I would like to suggest to you," or any other statement that would carry the same connotation.

And now let us begin in earnest our study of eschatology as revealed through His holy apostles and prophets throughout the ages. We will, for the most part, focus on the last book of the Bible, the book of Revelation. We will also include some of the Old Testament prophetic books that address the subject of eschatology. In so doing, we will compare our interpretation of such with the Olivet Discourse for congruency.

Overview of the Book of Revelation

Because our study will involve the use of many Scriptures from the book of Revelation, it is important that we have a basic understanding of this book. For this reason, we will now take time to give an overview of the book of Revelation.

There are three common fallacies concerning our ability to understand and interpret this book and end time events that need to be addressed at the outset of our study. They are as follows.

1. This book cannot be understood at this time.

2. This book does not apply to the Christian walk now.

3. This book is written in chronological order.

Revelation 1:1-3 should clearly convince us of God's intention that we understand this prophetic book and that these truths have been relevant to the Christian walk since approximately 95 AD.

> ¹The Revelation of Jesus Christ, which God gave Him to show His servants – things which must shortly take place. And He sent and signified it by His angel to His servant John, ²who bore witness to the word of God, and to the testimony of Jesus Christ, to all things that he saw. ³Blessed is he who reads and those who hear the words of this prophecy, and keep those things which are written in it; for the time is near. —Revelation 1:1-3

To help us understand this prophecy, especially with regard to its chronological order, we go to the key verse for this entire book, "Write the things which you have seen, and the things which are, and the things which will take place after this." (Revelation 1:19). John was instructed to write about the past (the things which you have seen), the present (the things which are), and the future (the things which shall be hereafter). This clearly divides this prophetic book into three parts. Revelation chapter 1 deals with the past, or what John had previously seen; Revelation chapters 2 and 3 deal with the then present condition of seven literal churches in Asia Minor; Revelation 4:1 shows that the rest of this book deals with the future, or things which must be hereafter. Since this book was written in approximately 95 AD, then all that is said after Revelation 4:1 speaks of that which takes place after 95 AD. This fact alone clears up much confusion that has been introduced in interpreting this book of the Bible.

The Story Told Twice

The one puzzle piece that needs to be added to understand the prophetic events of this book is that the story of the future is told twice. The first time it is told from God's perspective and the second time from man's perspective. The first time records the story as it would be seen from a heavenly viewpoint and the second time as it would be seen from an earthly viewpoint. I am not asking the reader to accept this premise without scriptural validation. And this we will offer in the following paragraphs and on numerous occasions throughout the course of this study. I just ask that you would be of an open mind like the Bereans.

Revelation chapters 4 through 12 tell the story from the heavenly viewpoint with various parenthetic passages interspersed throughout these nine chapters. Revelation chapters 13 through 19 begin the story again as would be seen from an earthly viewpoint interspersed with several parenthetical passages. Revelation

20:6–22:2 deals with the millennial kingdom, the great white throne judgment, and the eternal state.

One of the strongest arguments of the story being told twice as compared to one long, contiguous, chronological story is the impossible time constraint of fitting all these events into a seven-year period. If it is one long story, we must be able to fit seven seals, seven thunders, seven trumpets, and seven bowls into seven years. Many of these have time constraints that, when added together, would require much more than seven years. Allow me to offer just a few examples. How long would it take for the second seal to unfold, during which there will be wars (plural) that take place and rumors of other wars (plural) that threaten world peace? How about the four severe judgments of the fourth seal, in which one-fourth of the world's population dies? That doesn't happen in a matter of months. Or how about the fifth trumpet, in which locusts with scorpion stings torment men for five months? Or how about the sixth trumpet that covers a period of time of thirteen-plus months in which one-third of mankind will be killed by a 200-million-man army? Or how about the sixth bowl, where the kings of the East and all the kings of the entire world amass and stage a great army to surround Jerusalem? These are just five of twenty-eight events that must take place in a seven-year period. If the story is told twice, that would cut the number of events that must transpire at least in half.

Another major proof of the story being told twice can be seen as you compare the seven trumpets of Revelation chapters 8 through 11 with the seven bowls of Revelation chapter 16. They appear to be different. However, when one considers what each trumpet or bowl is affecting, it becomes obvious that these are speaking of the same events as told from a spiritual and natural viewpoint. The two together give us a more complete picture of what really is to take place in these future events. Don't let their apparent differences fool you and cause you to mistake these for two different series of events.

A good example of this biblical hermeneutic can be seen in another story told twice. Let us consider the story of the Roman centurion who had a sick servant he loved dearly, for which he sought help from Jesus. This story illustrates the need for a hermeneutic that rightly divides the word of truth. On numerous occasions where an account of a story is recorded in more than one book of the Bible, we see similarities but not total congruency between accounts. Knowing that each scriptural account is inspired by God, we need to take all the parts of each account and merge them together to get a more composite picture of what really took place. In the case of the centurion, most people in reciting the story tell of a centurion who went to Jesus and asked Him to heal his servant. When Jesus offered to go with the centurion to his house to heal the servant, the centurion said that he was not worthy to have Jesus come to his house. He then told Jesus that he believed if Jesus would just speak healing from a distance, his servant would be healed. When comparing the accounts of this story in Matthew 8:5-10 with Luke 7:1-10 and adding all the parts together, we can see that the centurion never went out to meet with Jesus personally nor did he ever speak to Him directly. Many Christians I have quizzed about this story only give the account from Matthew. It is not until we factor in the information given in the Luke account that we really get a more complete and accurate picture of what really transpired that day.

Another example of this hermeneutic is in the gospel accounts of the Olivet Discourse, where Jesus taught on eschatology.

There were three questions posed to Jesus by His disciples. Luke only addressed the very first question they asked concerning the destruction of the temple. Matthew and Mark were completely silent concerning this question. Luke talked about the coming tribulation of the Jewish believers and the destruction of Jerusalem in 70 AD. Matthew and Mark talked about the coming great tribulation at the end of the age. It is not until you add all the parts of all the accounts that you are able to see the big (complete) picture. This hermeneutical approach is worthy of your consideration as we continue our study on eschatology.

With this hermeneutic in mind, let us carefully examine the table on the next page, comparing the seven trumpets and the seven bowls. Hopefully, in so doing we might get a more complete picture of these seven events that will unfold in the future.

Trumpets & Bowls Comparison

Trumpet 1 ~ Rev. 8:7 Affects the earth, trees, & green grass	**Bowl 1 ~ Rev. 16:1-2** Affects the earth
Trumpet 2 ~ Rev. 8:8-9 Affects the sea, living creatures in the sea, & the ships	**Bowl 2 ~ Rev. 16:3** Affects the sea & living creatures in the sea
Trumpet 3 ~ Rev. 8:10-11 Affects rivers & fountains of water (fresh water supplies)	**Bowl 3 ~ Rev. 16:4-7** Affects rivers & fountains of water (fresh water supplies)
Trumpet 4 ~ Rev. 8:12-13 Affects the sun, moon, & stars	**Bowl 4 ~ Rev. 16:8-9** Affects the sun
Trumpet 5 ~ Rev. 9:1-11 Affects the bottomless pit or the kingdom of darkness (the throne & abode of Satan & his army)	**Bowl 5 ~ Rev. 16:10-11** Affects the throne of the beast or the kingdom of darkness
Trumpet 6 ~ Rev. 9:13-21 Affects the Euphrates River & prepares the way for an invasion by a vast army of 200,000,000 soldiers	**Bowl 6 ~ Rev. 16:12** Affects the Euphrates River & prepares the way for an invasion by a vast army led by the kings of the east
Trumpet 7 ~ Rev. 11:15-19 Affects the kingdom of God & the kingdoms of the world Citizens of the kingdom of God (dead & alive) are caught up into the air with the Lord to be rewarded for their works Citizens of the world remain on the earth to be punished by the wrath of God for their works	**Bowl 7 ~ Rev. 16:17-21** Affects the air, which is where the saints of God are caught up to meet the Lord Saints of God (dead & alive) are caught up to meet the Lord in the air —1 Thess. 4:17 Unbelievers are punished for their ungodliness by receiving the fierceness of the wrath of God

In comparing the trumpets and bowls, it would be hard to imagine that the exact same areas would be targeted twice in a matter of seven years! The *trumpets* give us a view of the seven events as seen from the spiritual realm as its counterpart *bowls* would from the natural realm.

The fifth trumpet and fifth bowl would be an example of the point this author is making. In examining these, let us pay particular attention to the target area affected by this trumpet and its counterpart bowl as seen in the Scriptures below.

Fifth Trumpet:

¹Then the fifth angel sounded: And I saw a star fallen from heaven to the earth. To him was given the key to the bottomless pit. ²And he opened the bottomless pit, and smoke arose out of the pit like the smoke of a great furnace. So the sun and the air were darkened because of the smoke of the pit. ³Then out of the smoke locusts came upon the earth. And to them was given power, as the scorpions of the earth have power. ⁴They were commanded not to harm the grass of the earth, or any green thing, or any tree, but only those men who do not have the seal of God on their foreheads. ⁵And they were not given authority to kill them, but to torment them for five months. Their torment was like the torment of a scorpion when it strikes a man. ⁶In those days men will seek death and will not find it; they will desire to die, and death will flee from them.

⁷The shape of the locusts was like horses prepared for battle. On their heads were crowns of something like gold, and their faces were like the faces of men. ⁸They

had hair like women's hair, and their teeth were like lions' teeth. ⁹And they had breastplates like breastplates of
iron, and the sound of their wings was like the sound of
chariots with many horses running into battle. ¹⁰They
had tails like scorpions, and there were stings in their
tails. Their power was to hurt men five months. ¹¹And
they had as king over them the angel of the bottomless
pit, whose name in Hebrew is Abaddon, but in Greek he
has the name Apollyon.   —Revelation 9:1-11

Fifth Bowl:

¹⁰Then the fifth angel poured out his bowl on the throne
of the beast, and his kingdom became full of darkness; and
they gnawed their tongues because of the pain. ¹¹They
blasphemed the God of heaven because of their pains and
their sores, and did not repent of their deeds.
                        —Revelation 16:10-11

Notice in each, the targeted area is the bottomless pit or throne
of the beast, which refers to the same area of focus. In both, the
atmosphere and sun were full of darkness. In the fifth bowl it
describes the condition of men as gnawing their tongues because
of their pains and sores. The fifth trumpet, however, describes
what was causing the pain. There were locusts with scorpion-like
stings in their tails, stinging all that were on the earth except those
who had the seal of God on their foreheads. Both accounts to this
point describe a very natural event. However, the fifth trumpet, in
describing the appearance of the locusts, begins to look at the spiritual activity that was behind and causing the natural judgment.
The description given of the locusts was not that of any earthly,
natural life-form. These were demons that were controlling the

locusts under the direction of the king of the bottomless pit, Abaddon, which is a Bible name for the devil. The natural viewpoint depicts men being stung by locusts, resulting in great pain. The spiritual viewpoint depicts what was happening in both the natural and the spiritual realms. The view from the spiritual realm shows the demonic forces directing and causing what was happening in the natural.

There are many other interesting analogies that can be drawn through a careful examination of each trumpet and its counterpart bowl. In analyzing these, it would be a real stretch of one's imagination to conceive of the notion that not only did lightning strike the same place twice on one of these events, but it would be even more difficult to conceive of this happening on all seven events. That is too much of a coincidence for this author. In addition to this, consider the amount of time it would take for these judgments to occur in each target area, the amount of time it would take for each of these areas to recover from the disaster, and finally, the amount of time it would take once again to bring the same judgment upon each target area. I personally believe the evidence overwhelmingly supports the fact that these judgments happened one time and that we were given two accounts of each event from two different vantage points.

With these things in mind, let us be open to the fact that the story of the future is indeed told twice. We will further substantiate and strengthen this fact later in this book as we repeatedly compare the events that are seen in both halves of one story. If this is true, it will have a significant impact on the ever-expanding development of your eschatological doctrine.

11

Understanding Death and Resurrection

Importance of the Resurrection

An integral part of eschatology are the doctrines of the resurrection of the dead and eternal judgment. Many Christians and non-Christians alike believe in one general resurrection and judgment at the end of time. However, this does not pass the scrutiny of the Scriptures.

The Bible clearly teaches that there are two resurrections and two judgments.

> [4]And I saw thrones, and they sat on them, and judgment was committed to them. Then I saw the souls of those who had been beheaded for their witness to Jesus and for the word of God, who had not worshiped the beast or his image, and had not received his mark on their foreheads or on their hands. And they lived and reigned with Christ for a thousand years. [5]But the rest of the dead did not live again until the thousand years were finished. This is the first

resurrection. [6]Blessed and holy is he who has part in the first resurrection. Over such the second death has no power, but they shall be priests of God and of Christ, and shall reign with Him a thousand years.   —Revelation 20:4-6

The first resurrection is finished before the millennial kingdom begins. All who are a part of this resurrection will rule and reign with Christ for a thousand years. However, the greatest benefit for the participants of this resurrection is that the second death will have no power over them. Accompanying this resurrection is the judgment seat of Christ in which the saints of God are judged and rewarded for the works that they have done during their earthly lifetime. The second resurrection occurs at the end of the millennial kingdom and before the final eternal state, after which time will be no more. Accompanying this resurrection is the great white throne judgment. In this judgment, the living will be divided by the Great Shepherd into two groups – sheep and goats or believers and nonbelievers. The sheep will inherit eternal life and the goats will be cast into the lake of fire where they will suffer everlasting punishment. Also judged will be the unbelieving dead who are resurrected and cast into the lake of fire. These had died in their sins and were already condemned (see John 3:18). The separation of the believing dead and unbelieving dead happens at the first resurrection where all the dead in Christ were resurrected to put on incorruption and immortality while the rest of the dead lived not until a thousand years later.

One of the proofs that substantiates the importance of the doctrine of the resurrection of the dead is Jesus' attitude toward those who pervert this doctrine and to whom He said, "you do greatly err" (Matthew 22:23-33; Mark 12:24-27; 2 Timothy 2:15-18; 2 John 7-11).

Another great passage that deals with the importance of the resurrection is found in 1 Corinthians 15:1-34. Here Paul reminds God's people of the gospel that he preached unto them, which they received and in which they stand. He further exhorts them that the genuineness of their salvation would be evident by their holding fast to the word that he preached unto them, which included the doctrine of the resurrection.

- In 1 Corinthians 15:3-8, he substantiates the validity of the resurrection of Jesus Christ.

³For I delivered to you first of all that which I also received: that Christ died for our sins according to the Scriptures, ⁴and that He was buried, and that He rose again the third day according to the Scriptures, ⁵and that He was seen by Cephas, then by the twelve. ⁶After that He was seen by over five hundred brethren at once, of whom the greater part remain to the present, but some have fallen asleep. ⁷After that He was seen by James, then by all the apostles. ⁸Then last of all He was seen by me also, as by one born out of due time.   —1 Corinthians 15:3-8

- So important was the resurrection to the message of the gospel that the devil came up with a very sinister plan to debunk the reality of its happening. This scheme to invalidate the resurrection of Christ was not the result of the devil working through a corrupt Roman government; it was conceived of by the chief priests and elders of Israel. They bribed the Roman soldiers guarding the tomb. They coaxed them to say that Jesus' disciples came while they were sleeping and stole the body. All of this was done to discredit the resurrection, to avoid being responsible for innocent blood, and to limit the growing number of followers who were believers in Jesus and His resurrection. What they could not control was the wisdom of God by which Jesus was seen alive by many witnesses after His death, burial, and resurrection.

- First Corinthians 15:12-19 further amplifies the importance of the resurrection by showing what adverse effects would exist if there was none. See below:

[12]Now if Christ is preached that He has been raised from the dead, how do some among you say that there is no resurrection of the dead? [13]But if there is no resurrection of the dead, then Christ is not risen. [14]And if Christ is not risen, then our preaching is empty and your faith is also empty. [15]Yes, and we are found false witnesses of God, because we have testified of God that He raised up Christ, whom He did not raise up – if in fact the dead do not rise. [16]For if the dead do not rise, then Christ is not risen. [17]And if Christ is not risen, your faith is futile; you are still in your sins! [18]Then also those who have fallen asleep in Christ have perished. [19]If in this life only we have hope in Christ, we are of all men the most pitiable.
—1 Corinthians 15:12-19

- If Christ is not raised from the dead, then there is no hope of a resurrection of those who died throughout the annals of time, even though they were believers. This would make the faith of God's people to be in vain.

- First Corinthians 15:20-34 clearly teaches the resurrection of the dead and its chronological order, with Christ being the very firstfruits.

The Nature of Death

Since there cannot be a resurrection without a death, it is important that one understands what really takes place when the death process occurs. To understand the death process, one must first understand that man is a living soul with a body from the earth and a spirit from God. The Bible teaches that man is not a spirit with a body and a soul. He is a living soul created with components from two different worlds, the natural world and the spiritual world. Therefore man is a living soul with a body from the natural realm and a spirit from the spiritual realm.

> 7And the Lord God formed man of the dust of the ground, and breathed into his nostrils the breath of life; and man became a living soul.   —Genesis 2:7 KJV

> 5And all the souls that came out of the loins of Jacob were seventy souls.   —Exodus 1:5 KJV

> 45And so it is written, The first man Adam was made a living soul.   —1 Corinthians 15:45 KJV

Death by God's own definition in James 2:17,20,26 is merely separation. Physical death is when our soul is separated from our body. Spiritual death is when our soul is separated from the spirit of God. If physical death occurs, it separates a living soul from the physical component of creation, which is dust or earth. If spiritual death occurs, it separates a living soul from the spiritual component of creation, which is the breath or spirit of God.

When a man dies, his body goes to the grave, his spirit goes to God, and his soul enters the eternal spiritual realm.

[19]For what happens to the sons of men also happens to animals; one thing befalls them: as one dies, so dies the other. Surely, they all have one breath; man has no advantage over animals, for all is vanity. [20]All go to one place: all are from the dust, and all return to dust. [21]Who knows the spirit of the sons of men, which goes upward, and the spirit of the animal, which goes down to the earth.

—Ecclesiastes 3:19-21

[5]For man goes to his eternal home, and the mourners go about the streets. [6]Remember your Creator before the silver cord is loosed, or the golden bowl is broken, or the pitcher shattered at the fountain, or the wheel broken at the well. [7]Then the dust will return to the earth as it was, and the spirit will return to God who gave it.

—Ecclesiastes 12:5-7

[34]Jesus answered and said to them, "The sons of this age marry and are given in marriage. [35]But those who are counted worthy to attain that age, and the resurrection from the dead, neither marry nor are given in marriage; [36]nor can they die anymore, for they are equal to the angels and are sons of God, being sons of the resurrection. [37]But even Moses showed in the burning bush passage that the dead are raised, when he called the Lord 'the God of Abraham, the God of Isaac, and the God of Jacob.' [38]For He is not the God of the dead but of the living, for all live to Him.   —Luke 20:34-38

Isaiah 42:5, Luke 20:34-36, and Luke 16:19-31 further substantiate this death process and also repudiate the commonly embraced theory of soul-sleeping while awaiting the resurrection of the dead.

The Nature of the Resurrection

Concerning the resurrection of the dead, it is a bodily resurrection only. The spirit and soul of man enters the eternal spiritual realm at death while only the body sleeps to await the resurrection. Soul sleeping is contrary to the teachings clearly set forth in the Bible. At death, the soul is far more conscious of far more realities than when it was in the body. Therefore, it is the body only that is resurrected and not our soul or spirit. The Scriptures teach there are two types of bodies, a natural and a spiritual, an earthly and a heavenly. In the resurrection, the natural earthly body puts on the spiritual heavenly one. We can see from the following Scriptures that at death only the body is sown into the earth.

> [35]But someone will say, "How are the dead raised up? And with what body do they come?" [36]Foolish one, what you sow is not made alive unless it dies. [37]And what you sow, you do not sow that body that shall be, but mere grain – perhaps wheat or some other grain. [38]But God gives it a body as He pleases.　　—1 Corinthians 15:35-38

> [42]So also is the resurrection of the dead. The body is sown in corruption, it is raised in incorruption. [43]It is sown in dishonor, it is raised in glory. It is sown in weakness, it is raised in power. [44]It is sown a natural body, it is raised a spiritual body. There is a natural body, and there is a spiritual body.　　—1 Corinthians 15:42-44

Philippians 3:20-21 says that God will transform our lowly body that it might be conformed to His glorious body. Luke 24:36-43 demonstrates some of the attributes of this glorified body we will one day put on. Some will put on this incorruptible body without ever dying. Those believers who are alive when

Jesus comes for His church will just be changed (exchange their corruptible body for an incorruptible body) to meet the Lord in the air with those who are raised from the grave (1 Corinthians 15:51-52).

This resurrection that we have been speaking of is the first resurrection. The second resurrection does not happen until a thousand years later. Both of these resurrections and the events surrounding them are described in Revelation 20:4-15.

12

The First Resurrection

Nature of the First Resurrection

Now that we have established there are two resurrections separated by 1,000 years, let us focus on the first resurrection.

The first resurrection is the sum total of all the saints resurrected prior to the establishment of the millennial kingdom. This event, where Jesus comes to receive His church unto Himself, is referred to in most Christian circles as "the rapture" or "the translation of the church." We will discuss this in greater detail later in this book.

Whereas most nonbelievers believe in one general resurrection and judgment, so many believers believe in one general rapture or translation of the church (all saints being translated at the same time). However, there is much disagreement as to the timing of the rapture. Some believe it occurs before the tribulation period begins; some believe it occurs at the middle of the tribulation period, and some believe it occurs after the tribulation period. The vast majority of those who believe in a literal rapture or translation of the church, however, would ascribe to either the pre-tribulation or post-tribulation camp. Though many have switched from one position to another in their search for truth, they all use Scriptures to support their doctrine. Let me remind you about a very important principle of hermeneutics previously discussed. The principle of which I speak is that whenever your position satisfies one Scripture and yet violates another, we must seek the Lord for enlightenment of a position that satisfies both. I have often been asked if I believe in a pre-trib or post-trib rapture. My answer to that question was and is, "Yes." Let me explain my answer.

I say this because I personally believe that all three positions have a measure of truth. Consequently, it is not an either/or proposition. The first resurrection is multi-aspected. Although we need more knowledge on end time prophetic events to deal with the chronology of the first resurrection, it is not necessary when dealing with the multiple aspects of this resurrection.

The following examples, though some are duplications, should be sufficient to provide more than enough proof that the first resurrection by necessity must have more than one aspect or catching away. Let us look at the multiple aspects of the first resurrection depicted in the Scriptures without trying to determine who these people are. All these examples describe those who are believers and therefore must one day be caught up to meet the Lord in the air as a part of the first resurrection.

- Christ is the very firstfruits of the first resurrection – 1 Corinthians 15:20-23. If there were no others raised until the rapture of the church, it would still mean there are at least two aspects of the first resurrection, since Jesus is most assuredly a part of the first resurrection.

- Some O.T. saints did come out of the grave the same day Jesus did – Matthew 27:52-53. These were resurrected from their graves after Christ but on the same day as Jesus. This means that there are at least three aspects of the first resurrection. On resurrection day, Jesus was the very firstfruit unto God, whereas the other saints were the firstfruits unto God and to the Lamb. I personally believe that these, like Jesus, put on incorruptible bodies and ascended with Him as a great cloud or assembly of witnesses.

- The manchild is to be caught up to heaven – Revelation 12:5. We will discuss who this manchild is later. However, we know this one was caught up to heaven after 95 AD and before the millennial kingdom. This, too, depicts another aspect of the first resurrection.

- The woman that is tribulated in the wilderness must be considered – Revelation 12:6-13. This woman is persecuted for 3½ years but overcomes the accuser of the brethren by the blood of the Lamb and the word of her testimony. She, too, is a believer and will one day participate in the first resurrection.

- The Gentile multitude that is depicted in Revelation 7:9-17 must be considered. These are they who have washed their robes and prepared themselves during the great tribulation period and therefore will be participants in the first resurrection.

- The 144,000 of Revelation 14:1-5 must be considered. These constitute the firstfruits of those redeemed from the earth from amongst men, as opposed to those firstfruits who are redeemed from the grave. And yes, these also will be participants in the first resurrection.

- The two witnesses of Revelation 11:11-12 are caught up to heaven. These are definitely overcoming believers, whether you believe these are two individuals or two corporate bodies of believers. Since they are believers before the millennial kingdom, they also will be a part of the first resurrection.

As I indicated earlier, some of these examples may be duplications, as the Scriptures speak of the same people on more than one occasion. Nonetheless, they indicate that the first resurrection is indeed a multi-aspected resurrection.

It is important to note that a multi-aspected first resurrection teaching cures three negatives that would otherwise result from teaching one general rapture. The first negative is that many don't believe it is important to know about most of the end time prophecies, since they do not affect them or apply to them. The second negative is that those who believe all Christians will escape the tribulation period results in a tendency to be without incentive to press into the kingdom now and, in many instances, to be slothful. The third negative is that those who believe they will go through the tribulation lack hope and incentive to strive for spiritual excellence now, since that will be accomplished when they go through the tribulation period.

Conclusions Concerning the Resurrection

Before delving deeper into the meaning of some of the Scriptures cited in this chapter, let us quickly summarize some of our conclusions concerning the resurrection of the dead.

1. The resurrection of the dead is not one general resurrection, but two.

2. The resurrection of the dead is a "bodily" resurrection only. This is true of both the first and second resurrections.

3. The resurrection of the dead is universal; it includes the righteous and the unrighteous, the living and the dead.

4. The first resurrection is multi-aspected. It is completed before the start of the millennial kingdom; the second death has no power over those who are a part of this one; all will appear at the judgment seat of Christ; all will rule and reign with Christ for 1,000 years.

5. The second resurrection occurs after the millennial kingdom; all the remaining dead shall be raised; the living and the dead will be present at the great white throne judgment; many will be cast into the lake of fire, which is the second death. The second death is eternal separation from the spirit of God.

13

Revelation 12 Study (part 1)

Revelation Chapter 12

Now let us begin an expository teaching of Revelation chapter 12. Our goal is to determine who and what the characters and events of Revelation 12 are, and how they are to unfold chronologically. Revelation 12 is a parenthetical passage that gives greater detail to what was spoken in the chapters previous to it (Revelation 4–11). Those chapters represent the story being told from a heavenly perspective. Revelation chapter 12 is probably the most important passage of the book in determining one's eschatological position. How you define the characters, the events, and the chronology of this passage will greatly influence your doctrine.

In defining the characters, events, and chronology, I would like to point out several facts that can be substantiated by any number of historical books, like Josephus, as well as Revelation chapters 1 through 4.

1. The book of Revelation was not written to Israel, but to Gentile churches in Asia Minor – Revelation 1:4,11,20;

     10:11 (not just Israel but many peoples, nations, tongues, and kings), and Revelation 22:16.

2. This book, according to most historians, was written by John the apostle, around 95 AD.

3. This book was to be a revelation to the church of that day, not only about eschatology. It was intended to give instruction in daily Christian living.

4. This book itself states in Revelation 4:1 that the events described in the remaining verses in this entire book happen after 95 AD.

Let us be careful not to violate any of these principles when interpreting the characters, events, and chronology of this passage of Scripture.

The Woman, the Child, and the Dragon

In the first six verses of Revelation chapter 12, John sees two great signs or wonders that appear in heaven.

First Sign or Wonder:

> ¹Now a great sign appeared in heaven: a woman clothed with the sun, with the moon under her feet, and on her head a garland of twelve stars. ²Then being with child, she cried out in labor and in pain to give birth.
> —Revelation 12:1-2

Second Sign or Wonder:

> ³And another sign appeared in heaven: behold, a great, fiery red dragon having seven heads and ten horns, and seven diadems on his heads. ⁴His tail drew a third of the

stars of heaven and threw them to the earth. And the dragon stood before the woman who was ready to give birth, to devour her Child as soon as it was born. ⁵She bore a male Child who was to rule all nations with a rod of iron. And her Child was caught up to God and His throne. ⁶Then the woman fled into the wilderness, where she has a place prepared by God, that they should feed her there one thousand two hundred and sixty days.

—Revelation 12:3-6

There are several interpretations as to who and what these characters and events are. Let us now carefully consider the characters and events identified in the above six verses in Revelation chapter 12 to understand their interpretation.

The First Wonder

The first sign or wonder is primarily about a woman. Some say the woman is Mary, the mother of Jesus. This cannot be true, for this interpretation violates one of the four principles we discussed earlier. Mary did not conceive and give birth to Jesus after 95 AD. Also, when Mary bore Jesus, He was not caught up unto heaven nor was Mary persecuted when she and Joseph fled to Egypt. Unlike the woman in Revelation chapter 12, she went to Egypt before her child was caught up to God and she was not persecuted in her wilderness flight but rather escaped persecution. However, the woman in this passage fled into the wilderness after her child was caught up to God and was there persecuted for 3½ years.

Some say the woman is Israel. They believe this Scripture was addressed to Israel and was about Israel. It is important to remember that in 95 AD, Israel no longer existed as a nation. In 70 AD the Romans led by Titus completely destroyed Jerusalem and the temple, took captive the Jews, split up their families, and scattered them throughout all the countries of the Roman empire. Their plan and intention was to forever destroy Israel's national identity and remove them from being a threat to the empire again. In 95 AD it would have been impossible for John to send what he had written to be read by a nation that did not exist. It was not until 1948 that God did the impossible by undoing the plans of man in restoring Israel as a nation to the very land from which she was taken captive. Israel once again became a nation, had a national identity, and had an address. On what basis can anyone make the assertion that what John was commanded to write was to be sent to Israel when it clearly states otherwise in what he wrote in Revelation 1:4,9,11,20 and Revelation 22:16? In addition, they also point to the fact that this woman had a crown of twelve stars, which represents the twelve tribes of Israel. They go on to assert that it was from this nation Jesus was born. However, this is a faulty interpretation for the following reasons. Israel was not pregnant with the Messiah after 95 AD. Jesus was not born of and into Israel after 95 AD. Israel did not flee into the wilderness to escape persecution after 95 AD. They had already been in captivity throughout the known world for some twenty-five years by that time. This book could not have been written to and intended for the nation of Israel.

However, John himself asserts that this book was clearly written to and addressed to the New Testament church. The seven lampstands in Revelation chapter 1 were interpreted by John as being seven churches. Revelation chapters 2 and 3 record seven letters written and sent to seven literal Gentile churches, and each letter was to be read by and considered to be relevant to all the churches. Do I need to remind you that this book passed the muster of canonization and therefore is still relevant and is to be read by all the believers of all the churches today?

This book is about the revealing of Jesus Christ and was included in the New Testament of our Bibles. Zechariah teaches that Israel, as a nation, does not recognize Jesus as their Messiah until they meet Him at the Mount of Olives at His second coming. They also do not believe in the validity of the New Testament, which means they would never get their message because they would never be reading the New Testament. Why would God send a message for Israel to the church which they do not believe in and expect them to read it in a book they do not believe in? Again I reiterate, "By what authority can anyone declare that this book was written about Israel or to Israel?"

If Israel is not the woman, who then is? I believe the woman is the church about whom it was written, to whom it was written, to whom it was sent, and by whom it was to be read. I will speak to this in more detail later in this book.

The Sun, the Moon, and the Twelve Stars

Before we begin to deal with what the sun and moon are symbolic of, let us consider the dual intent of the "Revelation." Without a doubt it is a book about eschatology. However, it is also true that it is a book to instruct Christians how to practically live their Christian life by walking in the Spirit. If it was only about eschatology, it would not have been a *now* word for the early church and therefore irrelevant to them. There would be no relevant prophetic words for them to read, hear, and keep. Christians were charged to keep the words of this prophecy, not just know its eschatology

(Revelation 1:3). This book has much to offer a Christian about seeing, entering, and living in the kingdom of God. This would seem to indicate that it was a book about practical Christian living as well as a primer on eschatology. The spiritual applications we draw from this book may differ according to the focus with which we approach it – the spiritual walk of the believer or eschatology.

Let us now consider the significance of the sun and the moon described in the first wonder. There are different interpretations as to what is being referenced by the sun and the moon. One position declares that the sun is a light source and the moon is just a reflection of that source. This is true. They then go on to say that this is a contrast between the sun which is God's law written on the hearts of His people and the moon which is the Mosaic law written on tablets of stone. They say that the church is clothed with the sun, which represents revelation, and that the moon is under her feet, which represents her not being under the law but rather above it. If the focus of this author was not eschatology, I would have no disagreement with this interpretation. However, since the focus of this book is eschatology, I would like to suggest another interpretation of the sun and the moon more applicable to our focus.

A major revelation of Jesus Christ is that He is the Alpha and Omega, the beginning and the end. I believe that in the Bible the revelation of Christ begins with Genesis and ends with the book of Revelation. In the beginning when He created the sun and the moon, it was said of them that the sun is the greater light that rules the day, and the moon is the lesser light that rules the night, or darkness.

The sun-clad woman is a depiction of the woman clothed or wrapped round about with the righteousness of Christ. A type and shadow of this can be seen in the tabernacle where all who enter through its gate are totally encompassed by the white linens, which is symbolic of being clothed with the righteousness of Jesus Christ. The lesser light, which is the ruler of darkness, is under her feet, where he should be. This is symbolic of the church being delivered from the powers of darkness, being translated into the kingdom of God's dear Son, and her subduing all God's enemies under her feet to be God's footstool. Positionally or legally speaking, these facts are already true. However, there are conditions of maturity the church must meet to make this an experiential reality.

As for the crown with twelve stars, could that not be a representation of the church built upon the foundation of the twelve apostles of the Lamb, who alone is the chief cornerstone? The church is the many-membered body that God promised Him if only He would die and allow His body to be sown as a seed in the earth. That seed is in all who by the Spirit are baptized into His corporate body through the new birth (1 Corinthians 12:12-14).

In addition, one last conclusion that can be gleaned from this first wonder is that the woman was not only pregnant but also in the throes of pre-birth labor pains.

The Second Wonder

In addition to the woman, the other main characters in the second wonder include a great red dragon with seven heads, ten horns, and seven crowns, and the woman's unborn male child.

³And another sign appeared in heaven: behold, a great, fiery red dragon having seven heads and ten horns, and

seven diadems on his heads. ⁴His tail drew a third of the stars of heaven and threw them to the earth.

—Revelation 12:3-4

Identifying the great red dragon is easy since he is clearly identified in Revelation 12:7-9 and Revelation 20:2. There is nothing left to speculation on this matter, since the Scriptures themselves tell us who the great red dragon is.

⁹So the great dragon was cast out, that serpent of old, called the Devil and Satan, who deceives the whole world.

—Revelation 12:9

²He laid hold of the dragon, that serpent of old, who is the Devil and Satan, and bound him for a thousand years.

—Revelation 20:2

Remember, the first telling of the story is from a spiritual perspective. That which is happening in the spiritual realm is rarely visible in the natural realm. The effects and results are visible, but most generally the spiritual entities causing them are not. How might this second wonder look and play out from a natural or earthly perspective? The answer to that question can be seen in Revelation chapter 13, which begins telling the same story the second time.

¹Then I stood on the sand of the sea. And I saw a beast rising up out of the sea, having seven heads and ten horns, and on his horns ten crowns, and on his heads a blasphemous name. ²Now the beast which I saw was like a leopard, his feet were like the feet of a bear, and his mouth like the mouth of a lion. The dragon gave him his power, his throne, and great authority.   —Revelation 13:1-2

In Revelation chapter 13, we see the rise of the beast from the sea of humanity. This is a world leader and his government. This beast gets his power, his throne, and his great authority from the great red dragon depicted in Revelation chapter 12. The time of the beast's emergence is definitely reserved for the last days. Revelation 13 depicts the rising of the beast into power. Revelation 12 depicts the satanically empowered beast after his rise to power. This further reinforces the fact that Revelation 13 starts telling the story all over again from a natural or earthly perspective. Notice that when the beast emerges in Revelation 13, he has seven heads, ten horns, and ten crowns. However, in Revelation 12 he only has seven crowns. Most readers assume that the events of Revelation 13 chronologically follow the events of Revelation 12. They conclude that three more crowns were added to the seven after the conclusion of Revelation 12. The real truth can be seen in comparing Daniel 7:7-8, 19-27 with Revelation 17:12-17. Here we see that the little horn (the Antichrist) was one of the ten horns that subdued three of the ten horns or leaders. There were still ten kingdoms (horns) but only seven rulers (crowns).

> [23]"Thus he said: 'The fourth beast shall be a fourth kingdom on earth, which shall be different from all other kingdoms, and shall devour the whole earth, trample it and break it in pieces. [24]The ten horns are ten kings who shall arise from this kingdom. And another shall rise after them; he shall be different from the first ones, and shall subdue three kings.   —Daniel 7:23-24

> [12]"The ten horns which you saw are ten kings who have received no kingdom as yet, but they receive authority for one hour as kings with the beast. [13]These are of one mind, and they will give their power and authority to the

beast. [14]These will make war with the Lamb.

—Revelation 17:12-14

From these Scriptures we can see that the stage where the beast has seven crowns is a later development than when he had ten crowns. This proves, chronologically speaking, that the depiction of the satanic-empowered beast recorded in Revelation chapter 12 is a later stage of development than that which is recorded in Revelation chapter 13. I want to reiterate that Revelation 12 completes the first telling of the story and Revelation 13 begins the second telling of the same story.

When it comes to eschatology, it is evident that God believes it is important for us as saints not only to know His plan for His people in the last days but also what the devil's plan is.

The Devil Is a Father but not a Creator

Often we see the devil steal from God's playbook because he knows it worked for God's team many times. He was not made in the image of the Creator like man and therefore is not a creator but is simply a copycat of those who are. There is nothing original about his plan; he simply counterfeits God's plan to serve his evil purposes. The dragon manifests as a satanic, empowered beast, which is like unto an evil incarnation of the devil himself. We see the devil following the same script as God. He is setting up his godhead and government to parallel God's. We know from the Scriptures that God has referred to Satan as a father. I believe that like God, Satan will incarnate as a manchild and do miraculous things by the spirit of antichrist. I believe he is on a course of mimicking God by setting up his unholy trinity. He is not the father of the true vine but is the father of the false vine; His son is not the

Christ but is the Antichrist; his spirit is not the Holy Spirit but rather is an evil spirit. Notice that the devil even copies God's plan of the death, burial, and resurrection of His Son, the male child, the Head over all.

> ³And I saw one of his heads as if it had been mortally wounded, and his deadly wound was healed. And all the world marveled and followed the beast. ⁴So they worshiped the dragon that gave authority to the beast; and they worshiped the beast, saying, "Who is like the beast? Who is able to make war with him?"   —Revelation 13:3-4

The above Scripture reveals the future plan the devil intends to implement. I believe the Antichrist will be an incarnate representation of the dragon. He will be given authority to rule and will be made head over all the kingdom of darkness on this earth. This governmental kingdom head will suffer a mortal wound and then be raised from the dead. The result of the counterfeit will be the same as with the true. Even as many throughout the world today follow and worship the risen Son of God, the Christ, so many throughout the whole world will follow and worship the Antichrist who died, was buried, and will have risen again. Is there any doubt that the devil will have earned his title of being a deceiver, a liar, and even the father of lies?

14

Revelation 12 Study (part 2)

The Woman Is the N.T. Church

If the woman is not Mary or Israel, then the only plausible option would be that the woman is the New Testament church, as we have stated in the previous chapter. I truly believe the woman in Revelation 12:1-2 is the church of Jesus Christ clothed with the Sun of Righteousness (Malachi 4:2) and the moon, the light that rules the night or darkness (Genesis 1:16), is under her feet where Satan ought to be. The church is impregnated by the Holy Spirit as was Mary; the child is born before the marriage is consummated as with Mary and Joseph. The physical union of Joseph with Mary did not happen until after the male child, Jesus, was born. So it will be with the woman and the manchild. She will give birth to her son before the church is united with Christ at the marriage and the marriage supper of the Lamb. As it happened with Mary, the mother of Jesus, so it will be with the church. As it happened with Christ, the head, so it will be with the body of Christ. The only difference is that what happened singularly or individually will happen corporately to this many-membered church.

Who Is the Manchild?

If the woman is a corporate body, so also is the fruit of her womb, the manchild. As it happened singularly with Jesus, so it will happen corporately with the manchild. Some would argue that this proves the manchild is Jesus because "Christ" is a singular word and "manchild" is, too. However, there are other words that are singular yet refer to a multitude, such as man when referring to mankind, the woman or the bride of Christ, the perfect man of Ephesians 4:13, and the reference to Israel as God's wife, not wives. These are but a few of the examples one could cite.

Who exactly is this manchild? If the woman is not Mary, then the woman's son cannot be Jesus. If the woman is not Israel, then the manchild cannot be a 144,000 overcoming Jews.

I believe that, like Mary, the Holy Spirit will overshadow the church (the woman of Revelation 12) and there will be a divine conception in which man has no part or contribution. The child within is the result of a spiritual seed being sown within through intimacy, not a natural seed sown through religion. Though this conception takes place inside the woman and is part of the woman, the new life within her is wholly a work of God. Though the woman and the child within are one, yet they are also two separate entities. These two will continue to live as one until the child within comes to maturity. When this child is completely developed, the time of separating these two will also come. I believe this is the first of two separatings that will take place within the woman, the church, in the last days.

The first separation has to do with the state of preparedness. It involves a clear demarcation between the church and an overcoming group of Christians within the church that will be a part of the corporate manchild. The purpose of this separation is to isolate a firstfruits harvest unto God and the Lamb of those who are alive on the earth. It is a separation not between virgins and non-virgins, but a separation of wise from foolish virgins. Even now, in this our day, discerning ones can see this separating process already in progress within the church.

The second separation has to do with personal identity. It involves a clear demarcation between true and false Christians, between authentic and nominal Christians. It is not a separation of maturity levels of one identity, but a separating of two distinct identities that look somewhat alike. Parabolically, it is a separation of wheat from tares. This will happen during the great tribulation. Jesus taught in the Olivet Discourse that those who confess Christ will be cast into great tribulation. Some will be a witness of Christ when tested and persecuted for His name's sake. However, Jesus said that many will deny Christ and be overthrown in this time of testing. Only those who endure to the end will be considered by God to be a part of the true church and therefore be saved.

The Firstfruits Manchild

If the rapture or harvest of the church is a reaping of both dead and alive, then the firstfruits of the harvest must include both dead and alive. The firstfruits must be reaped and offered unto God before the main harvest of the same is reaped. The firstfruits of the dead were reaped the same day Jesus rose from the dead. These as a great cloud of witnesses ascended and were offered unto God.

> [51]Then, behold, the veil of the temple was torn in two from top to bottom; and the earth quaked, and the rocks were split, [52]and the graves were opened; and many

bodies of the saints who had fallen asleep were raised; [53]and coming out of the graves after His resurrection, they went into the holy city and appeared to many.

—Matthew 27:51-53

The firstfruits of the living must also be reaped and offered unto God before the main harvest (rapture of the church):

[1]Then I looked, and behold, a Lamb standing on Mount Zion, and with Him one hundred and forty-four thousand, having His Father's name written on their foreheads. [2]And I heard a voice from heaven, like the voice of many waters, and like the voice of loud thunder. And I heard the sound of harpists playing their harps. [3]They sang as it were a new song before the throne, before the four living creatures, and the elders; and no one could learn that song except the hundred and forty-four thousand who were redeemed from the earth. [4]These are the ones who were not defiled with women, for they are virgins. These are the ones who follow the Lamb wherever He goes. These were redeemed from among men, being firstfruits to God and to the Lamb.   —Revelation 14:1-4

The identity of this 144,000 speaks of a group of people who are part of the circumcision, which is of the heart and not the body. It speaks of spiritual circumcision, not natural. It speaks of those who are born and matured by the Holy Spirit. Remember, Revelation chapter 13 begins the telling of the story the second time. But this is the manchild of Revelation chapter 12. Notice that they are not redeemed from the grave but from the earth. These will be redeemed from amongst men as a firstfruits unto God and the Lamb. It is interesting to note that they are referred to as virgins. I believe these are the wise virgins who are prepared, because they have their vessels full of oil. These are the same people who have learned to worship the Lord at the altar inside the temple. These are they that are being measured in Revelation 11:1-2. These are the inner court Christians who were counted worthy of escaping the forty-two months of tribulation into which outer court Christians will be cast (Luke 21:34-36). It is important to note that the determining indicator that differentiates the prepared from the unprepared is spiritual intimacy.

After the Manchild Is Born

When the manchild of Revelation 12:5 is fully developed, the woman gives birth and her child is immediately caught up to God and His throne. Like Enoch, this group of overcomers will be translated to be with the Lord without partaking of death. These, unlike Enoch, will put off their mortal bodies and put on immortal bodies. These will be the first to have put on their glorified bodies after Jesus and the firstfruits from the grave did. Immediately after this, the woman who gave birth flees into the wilderness where she is tribulated for 3½ years.

> ⁴And the dragon stood before the woman who was ready to give birth, to devour her Child as soon as it was born. ⁵She bore a male Child who was to rule all nations with a rod of iron. And her Child was caught up to God and His throne. ⁶Then the woman fled into the wilderness, where she has a place prepared by God, that they should feed her there one thousand two hundred and sixty days.
> —Revelation 12:4-6

Initially, the dragon was seeking to devour the manchild, not the woman. It is not until the dragon fails to devour the manchild before God catches him up to heaven that he turns his attention to the woman. God prepares a place of both testing and provision for the woman as she flees into the wilderness. Revelation 12:6 says that "they" feed her there for 1,260 days. I believe the "they" being referred to here is the many-membered voice of the manchild that was just caught up unto God. I believe that these overcomers, as saviors, will be commissioned by God to supernaturally provide for their brethren who are yet to overcome and put on their incorruptible, immortal, glorified bodies. Could Obadiah, verse 21, possibly be referring to the manchild coming to Mount Zion (the church) to save their lives by feeding her?

> ²¹Then saviors shall come to Mount Zion to judge the mountains of Esau, and the kingdom shall be the Lord's.   —Obadiah 1:21

A War in Heaven

In Revelation 12:7 it says that a war broke out in heaven. Many mistake this war for what took place before man was created, when Satan fell, along with one-third of the angels from heaven. A closer look shows that this war was not about Lucifer's fall from heaven, because he was not the devil or the dragon then. Neither was he the accuser of the brethren or the world deceiver then, because there was not a world or any brethren in existence at the time of his fall. Also, after that fall Satan was not limited to the earth. When comparing Job 1:6-7 with Revelation 12:7-10, we can see that Satan had access to the presence of God in heaven where he would go to accuse the brethren day and night. However, God challenged him about the life of Job, against whom Satan had no accusation. In addition, the war recorded in this passage had to happen after 95 AD on the basis of Revelation 4:1. After Michael defeated the dragon, he was cast out of heaven to the earth. He no longer had access to the second or third heaven but was limited to the first heaven, the earth. Again we remind you that this book was written to the Gentile churches and not the Jews (Revelation 1:4,20; 2:1). Israel's apocalypse was recorded in the Old Testament prophetic books of Zechariah and Isaiah chapters 24 through 27.

> [7]And war broke out in heaven: Michael and his angels fought with the dragon; and the dragon and his angels fought, [8]but they did not prevail, nor was a place found for them in heaven any longer. [9]So the great dragon was cast out, that serpent of old, called the Devil and Satan, who deceives the whole world; he was cast to the earth, and his angels were cast out with him.
> —Revelation 12:7-9

The dragon is identified as the devil and Satan, who was the deceiver of the whole world. Not only was the devil cast out of heaven onto the earth, but also all of his angels were cast out with him. In Revelation 12:10-12 we see the reactions of heaven and earth as a result of the outcome of this war.

> [10]Then I heard a loud voice saying in heaven, "Now salvation, and strength, and the kingdom of our God, and the power of His Christ have come, for the accuser of our brethren, who accused them before our God day and night, has been cast down. [11]And they overcame him by the blood of the Lamb and by the word of their testimony, and they did not love their lives to the death. [12]Therefore rejoice, O heavens, and you who dwell in them! Woe to the inhabitants of the earth and the sea! For the devil has

**come down to you, having great wrath, because he knows
that he has a short time.   —Revelation 12:10-12**

Let's look at heaven's response first. The reaction of heaven will
be that of rejoicing. I believe the loud voice heard in heaven is a
many-membered voice. One cannot help but notice from the use
of the words "our brethren" in Revelation 12:10 that this voice is
a corporate one and that all who were speaking were born-again
believers who were already in heaven. This is further substantiated
by the phrases "the kingdom of our God" and "the accuser of our
brethren." I believe this corporate voice is that of the overcoming
manchild company. Why? This corporate voice is coming from
heaven to which the manchild was just caught up and, in addition,
this many-membered voice rejoiced over the corporate woman left
behind because they were their brothers, and the accuser of their
brothers had just been cast down and limited to the earth. The
result of this fall is made clear in Revelation 12:10, which says,
"Now salvation, and strength, and the kingdom of our God, and
the power of His Christ have come." Before Satan's being strictly
limited to the earth, this had not yet become a living reality for
the church. Once Satan is cast down, the immature Christians left
on the earth will be made overcomers through tribulation testing. The saints will receive saving grace and supernatural power
to overcome in their time of testing. They will overcome their
accuser by rightly applying the blood of Jesus through faith and by
the word of their testimony, which they declare by faith. Even in
the face of death, they will not deny the name of Jesus. They will
be willing to give their lives for His namesake.

The earth will also be impacted by the outcome of this war.
The reaction of those on the earth will be that of dread and woe.

The devil, knowing that his time is short, will vent his fury and wrath on the inhabitants of the earth. He also knows that he has but a short time before he is chained in darkness for a thousand years during the millennial kingdom.

Revelation 12:13-17 expounds on how the devil and his armies will direct their rage, how long it will be vented, and upon whom it will be vented in the short time he has left to operate on this earth.

> ¹³Now when the dragon saw that he had been cast to the earth, he persecuted the woman who gave birth to the male Child. ¹⁴But the woman was given two wings of a great eagle, that she might fly into the wilderness to her place, where she is nourished for a time and times and half a time, from the presence of the serpent. ¹⁵So the serpent spewed water out of his mouth like a flood after the woman, that he might cause her to be carried away by the flood. ¹⁶But the earth helped the woman, and the earth opened its mouth and swallowed up the flood which the dragon had spewed out of his mouth. ¹⁷And the dragon was enraged with the woman, and he went to make war with the rest of her offspring, who keep the commandments of God and have the testimony of Jesus Christ.
> —Revelation 12:13-17

Upon being cast down to the earth, he immediately persecutes the woman who brought forth the manchild. The devil means it for evil, but God means it for good. The devil's plan is to punish the woman and spite God, but God's plan is to ready the woman. This is the great tribulation into which the church will be cast, that she might be tested and made ready. Remember, Jesus warned His people in the Olivet Discourse that they would be cast into great tribulation to suffer many things for His namesake. This wilderness testing will result in a great multitude of God's people coming out of great tribulation having washed their robes and making them white in the blood of the Lamb (Revelation 7:9-14). God will keep His people and nourish them for a time and times and a dividing of time, which is 3½ years or 42 months or 1,260 days.

When Satan, because of God's provision, can't get the woman, he then turns his attention to the remnant of her seed. Who could this remnant be? Who are these that keep the commandments of God and have the testimony of Jesus? If the church is untouchable, whom else would Satan want to come against to spite God? The only other people on this earth that believe in the one true God and His commandments are the Jews. Some would say that it couldn't be the Jews because they do not have the testimony of Jesus Christ. I would disagree because of what Revelation chapter 19 says.

> [10]And I fell at his feet to worship him. But he said to me, "See that you do not do that! I am your fellow servant, and of your brethren who have the testimony of Jesus. Worship God! For the testimony of Jesus is the spirit of prophecy.   —Revelation 19:10

This verse clearly says that the testimony of Jesus is the spirit of prophecy. The Old Testament is full of prophecies that the Spirit spoke to the nation of Israel concerning their Messiah who was to come. They rejected Jesus as their Messiah but that does not change the fact that these prophecies were speaking about the coming of Jesus to be their deliverer. I believe that the Jews satisfy the description spoken of concerning the remnant that Satan would turn against when he couldn't get the woman.

15

Comparing the Signs
with the Seals (part 1)

Introduction

In this chapter, we will begin to look at the chronology of end time Bible prophecies. Our purpose in this is that we might locate where we are currently on God's prophetic timetable in order that we might know for what and how we are to prepare. The main source of our information will be taken from the Olivet Discourse and the book of Revelation.

The Hour Is at Hand

Many Christians take the position that God deliberately wants to keep His people in the dark concerning the return of the Lord and the events preceding it. This could not be further from the truth. As we have stated before, part of the reason for the anointing is that we might preach the acceptable year of the Lord and the day of the vengeance of our God. The fact that God wants these declared is a clear indication that He does not want His people ignorant of these events. He also said in the Scriptures that He would provide signs in the heavens and in the earth as signals of the approach of the last days. The reason for this is so that His children would not be taken by surprise and that these times would not overtake them like a thief in the night. Today, God is calling His children to awake from their slumber that they might discern the signs of the times even as experienced people of the world can discern the signs of the sky.

Comparing Heaven and Earth

Now that we have taught some concepts concerning eschatology that are not widely taught in the church, let us begin to examine if these things are true in light of what Jesus taught on the earth. Remember, Section One of this book was devoted almost entirely to what Jesus instructed His disciples concerning eschatology while He was physically on the earth. His teaching was recorded in three of the four gospels in what is commonly referred to as the Olivet Discourse. John, the revelator, was the only gospel writer to not record the Olivet Discourse. He, the disciple that Jesus loved, received and shared what the risen and ascended Christ taught him from heaven. Remember in Section One we shared that whatever Jesus, as the Son of God, taught from heaven to the apostles and prophets must agree with what Jesus, as the Son of Man, taught His disciples on the earth. With that in mind, let us begin to compare John's heavenly account with the gospel's earthly account.

The Olivet Discourse and the Seals

In comparing the Olivet Discourse with the seals, we will use the Matthew 24 account with Revelation 6:1–8:6. In so doing, we will compare the seven signs we listed in Section One of this book with the seven seals of the book of Revelation. For your convenience, we have provided a table on the next page which compares the two.

Olivet Discourse Signs & Seals Comparison

1ˢᵗ SIGN ~ MATT. 24:4-5	1ˢᵗ SEAL ~ REV. 6:1-2
Deception and false prophets in the world deceiving mankind	White horse with rider going forth to conquer mankind after resurrection 1 Jn. 2:18-27 (antichrist spirit already present)

2ⁿᵈ SIGN ~ MATT. 24:6	2ⁿᵈ SEAL ~ REV. 6:3-4
Wars and rumors of wars affect the world, not just a couple of nations	Red horse with rider who had power to take away peace from the earth
WWI and WWII affected the entire world, not just a few nations	A time when men would kill each other on the earth
Many thought this would be the end of the world but Jesus said it wouldn't be	Speaks of war affecting the whole earth

3ʳᵈ SIGN ~ MATT. 24:7a	3ʳᵈ SEAL ~ REV. 6:5-6
Nation rising against nation not in war like verse 6 but in cold war for social, economic, & military supremacy	Black horse with rider carrying balances to measure daily food supply that costs a day's wages because of inflation
Cold war competition causes societal and economical upheavals which leads to hyper-inflation	Delicacies like wine are very costly but still available in times of inflation; not so in times of famine (where we are currently)

4ᵗʰ SIGN ~ MATT. 24:7b-8	4ᵗʰ SEAL ~ REV. 6:7-8
Prophetic fulfillment of the 4 severe judgments spoken of in Ezek. 4:12-23 (famine, sword, beasts, & pestilence)	Pale horse with rider who brought death to many through the 4 severe judgments
These are the beginning of the birth pains that give birth to the manchild (overcomers) of Rev. 12:2-5	One fourth of the world's population will die as a result of this seal opening
	This is the beginning of the birth pains

5ᵗʰ SIGN ~ MATT. 24:9-21	5ᵗʰ SEAL ~ REV. 6:9-11
The saints are tested & purged in the great tribulation for 3½ years	Souls of those martyred in the great tribulation are crying out to God
Many will be martyred for their faith	No more gospel invitation to "Come"

6ᵗʰ SIGN ~ MATT. 24:29a	6ᵗʰ SEAL ~ REV. 6:12-17
Immediately after the tribulation, there shall be signs in the sun, moon, & stars	Immediately after the 5ᵗʰ seal, there shall be signs in the sun, moon, & stars

7ᵗʰ SIGN ~ MATT. 24:29b	7ᵗʰ SEAL ~ REV. 8 & 16
Powers/authorities in heaven & earth are judged & shaken in the GDOGW	7 trumpets/bowls of God's judgment & great wrath are released on the earth

Comparing Sign 1 with Seal 1

Sign 1:

I encourage you, the reader, to take the time to compare Matthew 24:4-8 with Revelation 6:1 before proceeding. The first sign that Jesus gave His disciples (regarding their eschatological questions) was, "Beware of deception." These were the very first words out of the mouth of the Lord in response to their questions. He prophesied to them that many false brethren who say they are of Christ would come, and multitudes would be deceived by them. It should not come as a surprise to us that the deceiver would counterfeit that which was successful for Jesus. John 20:30 says that Jesus did many signs that people would believe and follow Him. These false brothers, operating under a false anointing, will also do signs to persuade many to believe in their message and follow them. This will happen even as the Lord prophesied. Paul told Timothy that there would truly be perilous times in the last days. I believe that the greatest perils of all will be those that are spiritual in nature rather than natural. Though we are to beware of men, we can only escape deception through spiritual discernment. Remember, Jesus said that if it were possible, even the very elect would be deceived. One of the most seldomly operated of the gifts of the Spirit is the gift of discerning of spirits, which includes both good and bad spirits. The only antidote for this spiritual attack is spiritual discernment, not intelligence or Bible knowledge.

Seal 1:

The first seal depicts the first of the four dreaded horsemen of the Apocalypse. I believe this seal also deals with deception resulting from the spirit of antichrist operating in the world through men.

> ¹Now I saw when the Lamb opened one of the seals; and I heard one of the four living creatures saying with a voice like thunder, "Come and see." ²And I looked, and behold, a white horse. He who sat on it had a bow; and a crown was given to him, and he went out conquering and to conquer.   —Revelation 6:1-2

I believe the unveiling of this seal began to happen very early in the history of the church, sometime after 70 AD (1 John 2:18-27). The ultimate consummation of this seal will be the rise to power of a literal Antichrist at the end of this age. Some people interpret the rider on the white horse as being Jesus. Jesus does sit on a white horse when He comes to this earth, but that does not happen until after all the seals, thunders, trumpets, and bowls are complete. His coming will be at the very end of this age. It will be heaven's final act to close out this age and usher in the new one. The first seal begins before the end of the age, during which an invitation to come to God is still being extended. When Jesus comes on a white horse, His weapon is clearly not a bow but rather a sharp two-edged sword. At His coming, the Son of God, not the Son of Man, is already the one and only true potentate. Therefore all authority is His, even as He informed His disciples before His ascension. This authority does not need to be given to Him again at the time of His coming. It is said of this rider that he goes out conquering and to conquer. Jesus comes to give life not by subjugation but as a matter of free choice. When we investigate the following seals and see their negative nature and activity, it is clear that though ordained by God, they are not authored or empowered by God.

Comparing Sign 2 with Seal 2

Sign 2:

The second sign that Jesus gave His disciples with regard to their eschatological questions was, "You will hear of wars and rumors of wars." Though there has always been wars and rumors of wars throughout the history of mankind, it was not until the early 1900s that there was a war that had universal or world-wide impact. It was and is referred to as World War I. Since that time the world has not known peace, nor will it ever again until the Prince of Peace comes to usher in the millennial kingdom. I believe all the signs and seals will have a worldwide impact. This is true whether we are speaking about the preaching of the gospel in all the world or whether we are talking about deception, wars, earthquakes, pestilences, or any other events revealed in the signs and the seals. However, Jesus also made it clear in Matthew 24:6 that when this particular sign happened, it was not signaling the end. In the first half of Matthew 24:6, He described the sign we are to be looking for, whereas in the second half He told us not to be troubled, terrified, or alarmed when we see it, because this sign is not a sign of the end. He said that the first two signs must come to pass, but the end is not yet. He goes on to list the signs that truly mark the end of the age and that must take place.

Seal 2:

I believe the second seal also deals with wars and rumors of wars. The second horseman is riding a fiery red horse and he has the ability to take peace from all the earth.

> ³When He opened the second seal, I heard the second living creature saying, "Come and see." ⁴Another horse, fiery red, went out. And it was granted to the one who sat on it to take peace from the earth, and that people should kill one another; and there was given to him a great sword.   —Revelation 6:3-4

This rider is also described as having a great sword, which is symbolic of war, and also as one having the ability to incite people to kill one another with the sword.

I trust by now that you can see that the signs that Jesus taught on the earth in the Olivet Discourse parallel the seals He taught John from heaven. It will be even clearer as we compare the remaining signs with the remaining seals.

16

Comparing the Signs with the Seals (part 2)

Comparing Sign 3 with Seal 3

Sign 3:

The third sign begins to list the signs that will truly signal the approaching of the end of this age, whereas the first two signs are the precursors that preface and lead to these end time signs. In this sign, Jesus told them that nation shall rise against nation and kingdom against kingdom. I believe this sign is competition between nations and kingdoms that leads to worldwide instability and upheaval. With regard to nation against nation, this is not speaking of actual war, as that would be a repeating of the second sign. I believe it is referring to cold wars where nations are continually strategizing against one another to gain superiority or even supremacy over the other. This has been happening on a global scale since World War II. There is even competition amongst nations who are allies. The goal of this competition is to gain economic, political, social, and/or military advantage over the other. For many years now nations have competed with and even spied on each other to gain supremacy. It is a fact that even allies have been caught spying on one another to gain advantage. However, Matthew 24:7 goes on to say that not only shall nation rise against nation but kingdom shall rise against kingdom. I believe that kingdom against kingdom is meant to be a contrast with nation against nation rather than a mere repetition. Kingdom against kingdom speaks of warfare and competition between spiritual kingdoms. I believe Jesus is talking about the kingdom of darkness rising up against the kingdom of light or the kingdom of God against the kingdom of the devil. There is ever increasing animus between the citizens of the kingdoms of light and darkness. Nations rising against nations and kingdoms rising against kingdoms lends itself to worldwide instability by unsettling both the natural and spiritual realms of man's existence. I believe, as in the case of Job, that spiritual entities were the perpetrators behind the activities and events that affected Job and his family. What happened to Job was both very natural and yet very spiritual in nature. So will it be as nations rise against nations and kingdoms against kingdoms in the last days.

Seal 3:

I believe the third seal deals with the worldwide repercussions and ramifications resulting from the competition between nations and kingdoms. It is a time of social, economic, political, natural, and spiritual instability and upheaval as a result of conflicts on two levels, the natural and spiritual realms.

⁵When He opened the third seal, I heard the third living creature say, "Come and see." So I looked, and behold, a black horse, and he who sat on it had a pair of scales in his hand. ⁶And I heard a voice in the midst of the four living creatures saying, "A quart of wheat for a denarius, and three quarts of barley for a denarius; and do not harm the oil and the wine.   —Revelation 6:5-6

Let us take a close look at the true meaning of Revelation 6:5-6. The subtopics often included with passages of Scripture in many Bibles title this particular passage as "Famine" or "Scarcity." I believe the Lord gave me specific revelation concerning the third seal that would contradict much of this popular thinking. He revealed to me that the third seal was about hyperinflation rather than famine. In famine, food and drink are in short supply and therefore not available to the masses. This would even include the finer things such as oil and wine. The rider on the black horse simply says it will take a day's wages to pay for one's daily sustenance. It is not that food is unavailable; it is simply very costly. I believe this is the result of the natural and spiritual competition that will eventually cause inflation to give way to hyperinflation. Notice that the rider on the black horse commanded that the spiritual entities that incited the worldwide competition would not harm the oil and the wine. This means oil and wine will be available during the unfolding of this seal. However, it will be too costly for the masses and only the few who are rich will be able to afford these luxuries. Whereas the third sign describes the cause of what will happen during this time, the third seal describes the condition resulting from this cause. I believe we are currently in a period of inflation that will quickly crescendo into hyperinflation. As we look at the prevailing conditions and activities of the economic, political, and social arenas of this world, it is easy to see that we are approaching the fulfillment of this seal at hyper speed. This world cannot maintain stability while countries are printing money to pay debt, while countries are quickly becoming more consumer-oriented than production-oriented, while countries are conspiring against one another for personal advantage, while countries are on an intentional course of eliminating the middle class (the backbone of every society), while countries lie to and deliberately deceive each other, while countries are ever increasingly turning their backs on God resulting in the degeneration of the moral compass needed to foster and preserve world cooperation and peace, and you could go on and on with other examples. While the nations are competing for social, economic, and political supremacy, the kingdom of darkness is competing with the kingdom of God for the souls of men. In my opinion, this is where we are on God's prophetic timetable.

Comparing Sign 4 with Seal 4

Sign 4:

As we have previously stated, one of the consequences of the clashing of both natural dominions and spiritual dominions is that these will precipitate severe conditions similar to the judgments God prophesied of in Ezekiel 5:17. Knowing the truth of God's immutability (unchangeableness) should also cause one to know that similar conditions result in similar judgments. We have Bible precedence of man's ability to pollute nature (the cause of the flood) and the devil's ability to pervert nature (the cause of the tornado that killed Job's children). In Revelation 6:7-8, Jesus confirms this by saying that after a period of time in which nation shall rise against nation and kingdom against kingdom, there will follow such things as famines, pestilences, and earthquakes throughout the entirety of the inhabited places. As previously stated, the word for "earthquake" in the Greek can refer to an earthquake or an upheaval or turmoil amongst people. Not only is the earth itself convulsing and reacting to all the ungodly practices and abuses, but there are also major upheavals and tremors socially, economically, politically, and spiritually. These describe much of what we are experiencing in this present world. Indeed, God says that before the end comes, nation shall rise against nation, kingdom shall rise against kingdom, and there shall be famines, pestilences, upheavals, turmoil, and death. These will be to such a critical degree that the entire world will reel under their impact. The Luke account adds to these signs that fearful sights and great signs shall happen in the heavens. These shall be of such a magnitude that people will be terrified by their happenings.

Seal 4:

The severity of the fourth seal will surely mandate that we know how to walk by faith prior to its unfolding. This seal is composed of the four severe judgments spoken of in Ezekiel 5:5-17 and Ezekiel 14:12-21, and now in Revelation 6:7-8.

> **7When He opened the fourth seal, I heard the voice of the fourth living creature saying, "Come and see." 8So I looked, and behold, a pale horse. And the name of him who sat on it was Death, and Hades followed with him. And power was given to them over a fourth of the earth, to kill with sword, with hunger, with death, and by the beasts of the earth.   —Revelation 6:7-8**

I believe the judgment in reference to the sword is not war but rather the violence and murder associated with man and beast's desperate attempts for survival during times of famine. Famine can produce great deviations from normal behavior in both man and animals. Because of hunger, men and animals will attack mankind. Because of death, there will be much pestilence. This seal could begin to unfold in our not-too-distant future and could constitute the shaking referred to in Hebrews 12:25-29. Try to imagine the spiritual, emotional, and physical fallout when one-fourth of the world's population dies during this seal. I believe that Psalm 91 might be referencing this very time period. It not only cites a time when thousands will fall at one's side and ten thousand at one's right hand, but it also gives wisdom as to how to be prepared for such a time as this. Read from Psalm 91 here:

> ¹He who dwells in the secret place of the Most High shall abide under the shadow of the Almighty. ²I will say of the Lord, "He is my refuge and my fortress; my God, in Him I will trust." ³Surely He shall deliver you from the snare of the fowler and from the perilous pestilence. ⁴He shall cover you with His feathers, and under His wings you shall take refuge; His truth shall be your shield and buckler. ⁵You shall not be afraid of the terror by night, nor of the arrow that flies by day, ⁶Nor of the pestilence that walks in darkness, nor of the destruction that lays waste at noonday. ⁷A thousand may fall at your side, and ten thousand at your right hand; but it shall not come near you. ⁸Only with your eyes shall you look, and see the reward of the wicked. ⁹Because you have made the Lord, who is my refuge, even the Most High, your dwelling place, ¹⁰No evil shall befall you, nor shall any plague come near your dwelling; ¹¹For He shall give His angels

charge over you, to keep you in all your ways. [12]In their hands they shall bear you up, lest you dash your foot against a stone. [13]You shall tread upon the lion and the cobra, the young lion and the serpent you shall trample underfoot. [14]"Because he has set his love upon Me, therefore I will deliver him."   —Psalms 91:1-14

Like the fourth seal, this passage describes a time in which the world will be reeling from the traumatic events that are shaking her. This shaking will affect all who dwell on the earth, both of man and beast. Notice it does not say that "Christians" will be exempt from what is happening and dwell safely. Rather, it refers to "those who have learned to dwell in the secret place of the Most High God." I believe many Christians will be casualties of the earth's shaking. Yes, they may still go to heaven, but in all likelihood it will be sooner rather than later, thus causing them to fall short of finishing the course that God had planned for their lives.

Before we move on to discuss the fifth seal, I want to discuss a common occurrence that takes place in the first four seals. At the opening of each one of these seals, one of the four living creatures in heaven who represents the four faces of God extends a gospel call to come and put one's trust in God. This invitation is offered to all the inhabitants of the earth as the antidote for what is happening as a result of that particular seal. Compare Revelation 4:6-7 and Ezekiel 1:5-12,28. I believe these four invitations to come to God are symbolic of the four gospels of the Bible. The four gospels present Christ in each of these four faces seen in the first four seals – Matthew presents Him as the King (the lion); Mark presents Him as the servant (the ox); Luke presents Him in His humanity (the man); John presents Him in His deity (the eagle).

Other events that I believe must happen in addition to the fourth seal before the opening of the fifth seal include the battle of Gog of the land of Magog in Ezekiel chapters 38 and 39, and the completion of the sorrows of Matthew 24:8.

More Reflections on the First Four Signs

God's direction to His people concerning the first two signs was to look for them but not be alarmed by them when they happen. They are not indicators of the end, just precursors. His instruction, however, concerning the last two signs covered in Matthew 24 is quite different. He says that when you see these signs, you are to look at these as the beginning of sorrows. The Greek word for sorrows in Matthew 24:8 is *Odin*, which means "birth pains." Other than the Olivet Discourse, this Greek noun is only used in two other Scriptures in all of the New Testament. As we shared in Section One, birth pains precede something new being birthed into our midst. Once they start, something new, unique, and never before seen is inevitably on the way. Let us take a closer look at the significance of these birth pains. These are the precursors of the coming of a very significant event in God's prophetic timetable near the end of this age. The event to which I am speaking is the birth and catching away of the manchild of Revelation chapter 12. In Revelation 12:2, the Greek word used for travailing in birth pains is *Odino,* which is the verb form of the noun *Odin* used in the Olivet Discourse. Remember, the great red dragon is waiting for the birth of the manchild so he can devour that which comes forth from the woman. He is waiting for the unveiling of the identity of the one who is being formed within the woman. Before birth there is only one recognizable identity, but after the birth there are two separate identities that are manifested. The dragon wants to devour that which is birthed, not that which is giving birth. Why? It is because his target is that which poses the greatest threat to his work. Though the true church has been born of the spirit of God, only those within her that learn to walk in the Spirit are a true threat to destroy the works of the devil even as Jesus was commissioned to do.

The manchild represents the wise virgins that were prepared. Though the church gives birth to the manchild, she herself is lacking oil (the anointing) by which empowerment comes to engage in effective spiritual warfare. It is for this reason the focus of the dragon is on the overcoming manchild. It is my personal belief that, even at this present time, the Holy Spirit is forming the manchild within the womb of the church. Currently, there is a separating taking place in the church of those who through much tribulation are pressing to enter the kingdom of God from those who avoid tribulation at all cost. The manchild consists of those who, like Paul, glory in tribulation. These know the value of enduring by faith the present sufferings and trials. They consider the trials they are presently experiencing as not worthy to be compared to the glory that shall be revealed in their lives. Overcomers will overcome the world. We must choose to do it now or wait until we have to do it during the great tribulation. Remember, tribulation is for the saints, not the ain'ts. Some Christians say that God would never place His people into such hardships. However, I would remind you that God chose for Israel the furnace of affliction as the means to purge them. In like fashion, it will be the instrument of God's choice to wash and prepare a great multitude from all nations, kindreds, peoples, and tongues to be a people of His own who will serve Him day and night in His temple.

17

Comparing the Signs with the Seals (part 3)

Comparing Sign 5 with Seal 5

Sign 5:

Now let us look closely at the Scriptures to see what happens after the birth of the manchild as described in Matthew 24:9-21. Notice that the very first word of this passage is "Then," which denotes what immediately follows the birth of verse eight. Jesus said, "Then they will deliver you up to tribulation and kill you, and you will be hated by all nations for My name's sake." Verse 21 refers to these times of tribulation, persecution, and testing as a time of great tribulation such as has never been before or will ever happen again.

> 21"For then there will be great tribulation, such as has not been since the beginning of the world until this time, no, nor ever shall be." —Matthew 24:21

Many scholars identify the recipients of this great tribulation as either being natural Israel or worldly sinners. They describe this tribulation as judgment for their unbelief and evil ways. Upon taking a closer look at this passage, however, we can clearly see this is not so. Israel, as a nation, missed the day of her visitation and rejected her Messiah. John said that Jesus came unto His own, and His own received Him not. The people Jesus is instructing in this passage are those who have received Jesus as their Messiah, resulting in their being ostracized and persecuted for His name's sake. Natural Jews and sinners will not choose to suffer for the sake of Jesus or His name. Many do not believe He is the Messiah and of those who do, many have not received Him as their Savior and Lord. This passage in Matthew 24 sounds similar to the Luke 21 account of the tribulation that Jewish Christians suffered shortly after Christ's ascension and before the destruction of Jerusalem and the temple. The Matthew 24 passage, however, refers to all end time Christians who have received the circumcision of the heart. This time it will be about the "Jerusalem which is above," which is the mother of us all.

> [24]...which things are symbolic. For these are the two covenants: the one from Mount Sinai which gives birth to bondage, which is Hagar— [25]for this Hagar is Mount Sinai in Arabia, and corresponds to Jerusalem which now is, and is in bondage with her children— [26]but the Jerusalem above is free, which is the mother of us all.
> —Galatians 4:24-26

Many Bible translations use the word "affliction" instead of "tribulation" in Matthew 24:9. However, the Greek word, *thlipsis* which is translated as "affliction" in verse 9 of many translations is the same Greek word used and translated as "tribulation" in

Matthew 24:21 and 29. Clearly, that which immediately follows the birth pains and the birth in Matthew 24:8 is the great tribulation period. The Bible declares that it will be of greater magnitude than at any other time in the history of this age. It is more than the world simply opposing us – we will be hated, not just disliked. There are Christians right now in Iran and China, to name two countries, who are already experiencing a period of tribulation. How can it get any greater or worse than being imprisoned, tortured, and/or martyred for His name's sake? There are pastors that have been executed in Iran because they will not renounce or deny Jesus Christ as their Lord and Savior. They would rather die for His name's sake than to deny Him. How can the conditions of the tribulation period be any worse than that? The difference is in the universal scope of tribulation, which indeed makes it the greatest tribulation period ever. It is "great tribulation," not because of the harshness of the treatment but the scope of the treatment. He is not addressing this teaching to a few disciples or a few countries. His target audience in this passage of Scripture is the entire Christian faith. All those who know or say that they believe in Jesus Christ will be hated. Why? They will be hated for His name's sake.

Many of those being tribulated will be overthrown in the wilderness testing, even as was the case with natural Israel in her wilderness testing. This is clearly borne out in Israel's biblical history, which can be seen in Hebrews chapter 3. God said He was not well-pleased with many of them because they were overthrown in the wilderness. Some of us who are professing Christians today are being subjected to wilderness testings even before this time of great tribulation. God will not be pleased with us either if we are overthrown and overcome by the very test that He has purposed to prepare, build, and equip our lives. Nonetheless, God has reserved the great tribulation for those who avoided or failed times of testing previously. It will be a time and means for Christians in the last days to be thoroughly purged and made ready as overcomers. This will not be germane to a group of isolated Christians in a few isolated countries, but will be relevant to all Christians of all nations, tribes, peoples, and tongues.

> [9]After these things I looked, and behold, a great multitude which no one could number, of all nations, tribes, peoples, and tongues, standing before the throne and before the Lamb, clothed with white robes, with palm branches in their hands, [10]and crying out with a loud voice, saying, "Salvation belongs to our God who sits on the throne, and to the Lamb!" [11]All the angels stood around the throne and the elders and the four living creatures, and fell on their faces before the throne and worshiped God, [12]saying: "Amen! Blessing and glory and wisdom, thanksgiving and honor and power and might, be to our God forever and ever. Amen."
>
> [13]Then one of the elders answered, saying to me, "Who are these arrayed in white robes, and where did they come from?" [14]And I said to him, "Sir, you know." So he said to me, "These are the ones who come out of the great tribulation, and washed their robes and made them white in the blood of the Lamb."   —Revelation 7:9-14

The world system under the direct influence of the devil and his demons will be out to eradicate the church. It will be the same spirit that influenced Adolph Hitler to be consumed with exterminating the Jews. Why this hatred? It is because the devil and his demons hate God and those God has chosen to be the apple of His eye. Satan knows the church is God's instrument of choice to usher in the kingdom of God on this earth. The beast, the one-world government of the last days, will declare war on the church universal no matter what the denomination or affiliation. Both nominal Christians and genuine Christians alike will be cast into the great tribulation. Though the one-world system will not be able to discern between the true and false, God will. He will use this time of severe wilderness testing to separate the false from the true, the goats from the sheep. That which undergoes tribulation will respond in one of two ways – confessing the lordship of Jesus Christ for His name's sake, or denying it. How will this happen?

Matthew 24:10 clearly speaks to this question. The means God will use to separate the true church from the false church is by their response to the very tribulation into which they are cast. Some will by faith endure the tribulation and many others will be offended. They will be overthrown and forsake the Lord and also forsake those who are truly His. The offended will align themselves with and pledge allegiance to the one-world empire to escape the persecution being imposed upon them. In so doing, they make themselves the enemies of the cross of Christ and partners with those who are the enemies of Christ and His true church. This makes them partners with and every bit as anti-Christ as the very Antichrist himself. The Greek word for "offended" in Matthew 24:10 is *skandalidzo*. The definition of this word means to be scandalized, entrapped, enticed to sin, to fall into apostasy, or to fall into the displeasure of the Lord. This leads to the betrayal of the offended ones' natural and spiritual families. Betrayal such as this should never be found in the church, which is to be God's "holy place." And how will many be persuaded to switch their allegiance? It will be because of fear, their lack of spiritual discernment, and their lack of sound judgment caused by allowing their love for the Lord to grow cold. They will succumb to deception and be overthrown by the many false prophets who will come with signs and wonders following their ministries. Only those who endure to the end of these testings will be saved. I believe the love of many growing cold, generally speaking, is emblematic of the Laodicean age of the dispensation of the New Testament church. The letters written to the seven churches in Revelation chapters 2 and 3 were representative of the current conditions and state of those churches in 95 AD. I believe the Scriptures were typologically fulfilled with these seven literal churches. However, I believe the Scriptures represent a more prophetic fulfillment by the depiction of the various stages of the church from its inception to the end of the age. I also believe that during every stage or phase there were some who were better represented by one of the other seven church descriptions. For example, even though generally speaking the church today is best represented by the letter to Laodicea, there are some Christians such as in Iran and China who would be better represented by the letter to Smyrna. Smyrna was a church in the midst of severe tribulation and persecution. Though some Christians may be better represented by one of the other six phases from Ephesus to Philadelphia, generally speaking, most will be in the Laodicean spiritual state in the last days. They will be totally oblivious to their spiritual poverty. They will think that they are rich when they are really poor. They will think that they are hot when they are really cold. This makes them lukewarm in the eyes of the Lord. Even in this state, the Lord is faithful to reach out to deliver them. He will do this by chastening those He loves. For those who respond to the chastening of the Lord, He will be faithful to knock at the door of their hearts, promising to come in if only they will open up to Him.

For those who recognize their spiritual poverty and have followed God's counsel to buy gold, white raiment, and eye salve, the Lord will help them greatly to endure this time of severe testing and great tribulation. The prevailing hardships that will cause many to deny Him will also cause some to be a witness for the Lord. This will result in an effectual preaching of the gospel in all the world by both their faithful words and their faithful actions. For many, the cost will be their very lives; some will be martyred. After the gospel has been effectively preached and demonstrated, then the end of the age will begin to approach rapidly like dominoes falling one right after another.

The life and death of Jesus serves as a model of spreading the gospel of the kingdom in such a manner. Consider the day He died. How did He preach the gospel that day? Apparently His life and actions were enough to convince the thief on the cross that He was real. Without any Bible teaching from Jesus, the thief understood that Jesus was a King and that today He was going to return to His kingdom. Jesus' life and actions were such a witness of the good news of the gospel of the kingdom that the thief acknowledged he was a sinner and Jesus was innocent. He then asked Jesus to remember him when He came into His kingdom. So effective was Jesus' preaching of the gospel that day that a vile sinner was converted and received eternal life. Jesus confirmed his conversion by saying, "Today you will be with Me in paradise" (Luke 23:43).

I am not inferring that you have to die to be a witness. The Greek word for witness, however, is *martys* from which we get the word "martyr." You can be a witness of the gospel of the kingdom without dying naturally, but not without dying. The dying I am referring to is that of dying to your own self interests in order to serve life to others. These are they of whom it is written, "They loved not their lives unto the death" (Revelation 12:11 KJV). These are they who overcame by the blood of the Lamb and the word of their testimony.

> [7]But we have this treasure in earthen vessels, that the excellence of the power may be of God and not of us. [8]We are hard-pressed on every side, yet not crushed; we are perplexed, but not in despair; [9]persecuted, but not forsaken; struck down, but not destroyed– [10]always carrying about in the body the dying of the Lord Jesus, that the life of Jesus also may be manifested in our body. [11]For we who live are always delivered to death for Jesus' sake, that the life of Jesus also may be manifested in our mortal flesh. [12]So then death is working in us, but life in you. [13]And since we have the same spirit of faith, according to what is written, "I believed and therefore I spoke," we also believe and therefore speak. —2 Corinthians 4:7-13

Those who overcome understand that God is in control and that He is the Sovereign Potentate. They understand that the devil has no authority or ability to displace God's predetermined plan for their lives and that God's sovereignty is not in the least bit challenged by or subject to what the devil is attempting to do in their lives. As a matter of fact, they believe that the devil is subject to what God is doing in their lives through the faith and trust they place in the Almighty God.

We, too, of this last generation, are challenged to be overcomers even in the midst of severe testing. We are able to do this by our right appropriation of the blood of the Lamb and the word of our testimony. God promises His children that if we truly believe, He will never put us into a test that is greater than what we are able to stand or bear, but will with the temptation provide us the way of escape that we may be able to bear it.

> ^{13}No temptation has overtaken you except such as is common to man; but God is faithful, who will not allow you to be tempted beyond what you are able, but with the temptation will also make the way of escape, that you may be able to bear it.   —1 Corinthians 10:13

The issue is not whether or not we have trials and tests; the issue is how are we going to respond to those trials and tests that He declares are common to all of mankind. Everyone goes through these things. We must understand that God has purposed tribulation not for the "ain'ts" but for the "saints." There is something about tribulation that makes us press harder into the kingdom of God. It teaches us something of great value. There is a vital lesson to be learned. That's why Paul said to the churches, "We must through many tribulations enter the kingdom of God" (Acts 14:22). That is why Paul also said in Romans 5:3-5 that he gloried in tribulations. He would never glory and value punishment or judgment. Tribulation offers a positive hope and outcome. Judgment does not!

Some teachers say that God would never cast any of His children that He so dearly loves into tribulation. This is totally contrary to the Scriptures. Again I feel it important to remind you that throughout the ages of God dealing with His people, He has never been hesitant to lead His children into the wilderness to be tested or tribulated. He has often chosen the furnace of affliction for His children. We must understand that the purpose of the tribulation period is to be a time of testing and preparation, not a time of judgment. We will talk about the time of judgment that

God has reserved for the unbelievers of this world later in this section of the book. It is referred to as the great day of God's wrath.

Seal 5:

As we compare the signs Jesus taught in the Olivet Discourse with the seals that Jesus taught John in the book of Revelation, it should be evident by now that they are tracking congruently. This should not surprise us, considering Jesus was teaching on the same topic in both venues. Jesus would not teach something from heaven that would contradict what He taught His disciples on the earth. If you haven't been totally convinced by the comparison of the first four signs and seals, the fifth and sixth signs and seals should make a believer of you.

First let me share a revelation I received over 30 years ago as I was studying the seven seals. The Lord suddenly revealed to me that the fifth seal was the great tribulation. That sent me on a quest to see if I could from the Scriptures substantiate what I felt He spoke. When receiving revelation, we must always test who the speaker is as well as the message. This is what Jesus did when He was tested in the wilderness. He used the Scriptures to test what was being spoken to Him, and we should do no less. What God currently speaks will never contradict what He has spoken in the Scriptures. Let us take a look at the fifth seal and other supporting Scriptures to see if the revelation I received is truly of the Lord.

> [9]When He opened the fifth seal, I saw under the altar the souls of those who had been slain for the word of God and for the testimony which they held. [10]And they cried with a loud voice, saying, "How long, O

Lord, holy and true, until You judge and avenge our blood on those who dwell on the earth?" [11]Then a white robe was given to each of them; and it was said to them that they should rest a little while longer, until both the number of their fellow servants and their brethren, who would be killed as they were, was completed.   —Revelation 6:9-11

As the fifth seal opened, John saw the souls of many who had been martyred throughout the ages. These were already under the altar prior to the opening of this seal. These asked the Lord how long it would be before He would avenge them. The Lord's response was that they would have to wait a little while longer, until others who were to join them in martyrdom would be killed during this fifth seal. Jesus taught His disciples that immediately after the fourth sign they would be delivered up unto tribulation and killed. The same is also true immediately following the fourth seal. The fifth seal clearly depicts those who would be slain for the Word of God and for the testimony they held, even as the slain ones under the altar. Those who are yet to be martyred are the ones depicted in Revelation chapter 12 who, when tested for their faith, overcome by the blood of the Lamb and the word of their testimony. These not only confess the name of Jesus when called before officials, they even love not their lives unto death. Revelation 13:15-16 says that the satanic-empowered beast will be given power to kill all who will not worship the image of the beast and receive his mark on their right hands or foreheads.

In the next chapter, we will look at other supporting Scriptures to continue testing the revelation I received concerning the fifth seal.

18

Comparing the Signs with the Seals (part 4)

Comparing Sign 6 with Seal 6

Sign 6:

We showed you from the Scriptures that the fifth sign would be God's children being cast into great tribulation to be tried for their faith. There is nothing ambiguous about the sixth sign, as the Scriptures clearly identify what happens immediately after the great tribulation.

> [29]"Immediately after the tribulation of those days the sun will be darkened, and the moon will not give its light; the stars will fall from heaven, and the powers of the heavens will be shaken. [30]Then the sign of the Son of Man will appear in heaven, and then all the tribes of the earth will mourn, and they will see the Son of Man coming on the clouds of heaven with power and great glory.
> —Matthew 24:29-30

There is no great mystery here. The sign immediately following the great tribulation is that the sun, moon, stars, and even the principalities and powers of the heavens will be shaken and affected. Then the inhabitants of the earth and the principalities in heavenly places will see in heaven the sign of the coming of the Son of Man with power and great glory. All the tribes of the earth will mourn when they see this sign. The Luke account of this same event indicates that men's hearts will fail them for fear of the things that are about to come to pass on this earth.

> [25]"And there will be signs in the sun, in the moon, and in the stars; and on the earth distress of nations, with perplexity, the sea and the waves roaring; [26]men's hearts failing them from fear and the expectation of those things which are coming on the earth, for the powers of the heavens will be shaken. [27]Then they will see the Son of Man coming in a cloud with power and great glory.
> —Luke 21:25-27

I believe the fear in the hearts of men will be because the Lord reveals that He is about to pour out His wrath and judgments on the inhabitants of this earth.

Now let us compare this sign with the sixth seal.

Seal 6:

When the sixth seal is opened, we see the same areas being affected as those in the sixth sign. The sixth sign and the sixth seal are clearly speaking of the same event.

> [12]I looked when He opened the sixth seal, and behold, there was a great earthquake; and the sun became black as sackcloth of hair, and the moon became like blood. [13]And

the stars of heaven fell to the earth, as a fig tree drops its late figs when it is shaken by a mighty wind. [14]Then the sky receded as a scroll when it is rolled up, and every mountain and island was moved out of its place. [15]And the kings of the earth, the great men, the rich men, the commanders, the mighty men, every slave and every free man, hid themselves in the caves and in the rocks of the mountains, [16]and said to the mountains and rocks, "Fall on us and hide us from the face of Him who sits on the throne and from the wrath of the Lamb! [17]For the great day of His wrath has come, and who is able to stand.

—Revelation 6:12-17

This seal is an announcement of the coming judgment. The seventh seal is the unfolding of that judgment. The sixth seal has more to do with the terror that pierces the hearts of men before the wrath of God is released than it does on the judgment itself. Sometimes, the fear and terror preceding death is worse than the death itself. I believe this will cause such a fear and dread to come upon men that the hearts of some will fail them even as Jesus taught His disciples. At this point in time, all will know who the Lamb of God is, even though the seventh seal has yet to be opened. All will know that the great day of His wrath is about to come upon them.

In this seal we see the coming of the Lord, but this is not His second coming. Neither is it His coming for the church at the rapture. Though He pours out His judgments on the earth, He does not actually physically touch down on the earth until the great day of His wrath is finished. It is important that we separate His coming at the day of the Lord, His coming at the rapture, and His coming at the return or second coming of the Lord.

His literal second coming, during which He establishes the millennial kingdom, does not happen until approximately 3½ years after the announcement of the day of the Lord. We will go into greater detail on this when we cover the seventh seal.

The Day of the Lord

There are a number of Scriptures that speak of the day of the Lord in addition to the sixth seal of Revelation chapter 6. I have included a couple of these passages below from Zephaniah and Isaiah. (For your convenience, I have included in Appendix A many other scriptural references concerning this topic of the day of the Lord.)

> [14]The great day of the Lord is near, it is near, and hastens greatly, even the voice of the day of the Lord: the mighty man shall cry there bitterly. [15]That day is a day of wrath, a day of trouble and distress, a day of wastedness and desolation, a day of darkness and gloominess, a day of clouds and thick darkness, [16]a day of the trumpet and alarm against the fenced cities, and against the high towers. [17]And I will bring distress upon men, that they shall walk like blind men, because they have sinned against the Lord: and their blood shall be poured out as dust, and their flesh as the dung. [18]Neither their silver nor their gold shall be able to deliver them in the day of the Lord's wrath; but the whole land shall be devoured by the fire of his jealousy: for he shall make even a speedy riddance of all them that dwell in the land.
>
> —Zephaniah 1:14-18 KJV

> [6]Howl ye; for the day of the Lord is at hand; it shall come as a destruction from the Almighty. [7]Therefore shall all

hands be faint, and every man's heart shall melt: ^{8}And they shall be afraid: pangs and sorrows shall take hold of them; they shall be in pain as a woman that travails: they shall be amazed one at another; their faces shall be as flames. ^{9}Behold, the day of the Lord cometh, cruel both with wrath and fierce anger, to lay the land desolate: and he shall destroy the sinners thereof out of it. ^{10}For the stars of heaven and the constellations thereof shall not give their light: the sun shall be darkened in his going forth, and the moon shall not cause her light to shine. ^{11}And I will punish the world for their evil, and the wicked for their iniquity; and I will cause the arrogance of the proud to cease, and will lay low the haughtiness of the terrible.   —Isaiah 13:6-11 KJV

It is important to note that there is nothing redemptive about the day of the Lord. It is not about turning the hearts of men unto repentance. It is about punishing those who have troubled the earth with their wicked ways. The scope of the day of the Lord will not be localized to a nation or several nations – it will be universal. It will affect all nations, kindreds, and tongues.

What Precedes the Day of the Lord?

Jesus told His disciples that the day of the Lord would happen immediately after the great tribulation. This means that the great tribulation is the event that precedes the day of the Lord. Why is this important? It becomes significant when we are trying to identify the fifth and sixth seals. Since the sixth seal is the day of the Lord and the event that immediately precedes it is the fifth seal, then the fifth seal must be the great tribulation.

This poses an interesting question about the timing of the seals. Since the fifth seal is the great tribulation, that means the first four seals must take place before the great tribulation, not during it. This debunks the popular eschatological theology of the day which believes that all the seals, all the trumpets, and all the bowls occur during the seven-year tribulation period. This assumption cannot be substantiated by the Scriptures. This has been the basis of most eschatological teachings for years. If one's initial premise and foundation upon which you build your theology is faulty, then all that is built upon it will be faulty. Issues of timing concerning the fulfillment of end time prophecies have created several camps of thinking on this matter. Whereas the "preterists" believe that all end time prophecies have already taken place, the "futurists" believe that all end time prophecies are yet to happen. I believe the balance between these two extremes would be in the camp of the "presentists." These believe that end time prophecies are presently unfolding. This means some have happened, some are happening now, and some will happen in the future. I believe this camp allows us to get a more accurate read as to where we presently are on God's prophetic timetable.

Where Are We?

To ascertain where we are, we must first determine what has happened and what needs to happen in the future to satisfy the Scriptures. Let us look at the signs and seals to determine those end time prophecies that have already happened. The Luke account of the Olivet Discourse clearly states that before any of the signs take place, Jerusalem would fall and God's people would be scattered throughout the world. This means that none of the signs or seals could unfold before the destruction of Jerusalem in 70 AD.

The first sign and seal has to do with conquering the souls of men through deception. I believe the spirit of antichrist, as depicted in the first seal, was released into the earth sometime after 70 AD and before the writing of John's first epistle in approximately 90-95 AD. John declared in his first epistle that even though the Antichrist would come in the future, there were already many antichrists manifesting in the churches. He declared that the anointing we have received from God is the antidote against deception (1 John 2:18-27). This has already happened and is continuing.

The second sign and seal has to do with wars and rumors of wars. Since all the signs and seals will have a universal worldwide effect, this is referring to the two world wars and those whose similar impact would follow. The second seal emphasizes this universal effect by declaring that the rider on the red horse will have power to take peace from the earth, not just from several countries. This has already happened in part, and the rumors of more to come are continuously swirling around us.

The third sign and seal, I am persuaded, has to do with hyper-inflation brought on by competition between nations (natural) and kingdoms (spiritual) as a result of their selfish interests and agendas. The third seal declares that it will take a day's wages just to meet the essential needs to survive and sustain one's life. Though the essentials of life are very costly today, the worst is yet to come. Though inflation has been occurring steadily since the advent of the two world wars, it has yet to reach the critical mass that was prophesied. The lack of true cooperation between nations will result in a soon coming hyperinflation. I believe the world is on the brink of an unprecedented economic collapse. This could happen rapidly with just one or two worldwide calamities, be it man-made

or a natural disaster. Another contributing cause behind this imminent worldwide catastrophe is the ongoing and ever increasing animus between spiritual kingdoms. I personally believe that we are
currently in the midst of the unfolding of this seal.

The fourth sign and seal has yet to happen. During the
unfolding of this seal, one-fourth of the world's population will
die because of the four severe judgments that will befall this earth
and those who dwell thereon. Needless to say, the fifth through
seventh seals must also be fulfilled before the end of this age.

Considering where we are on God's prophetic timetable, how
expedient is it that all of God's children be sober-minded and prepare ourselves to be overcomers in such troublesome times as are
soon approaching?

19

The Great Day
of God's Wrath

The Pause Before the Wrath

Before we begin to deal with the actual unfolding of the great day of wrath, let us consider a question posed at the end of the sixth seal.

> [17]"For the great day of His wrath has come, and <u>who is able to stand?</u>"   —Revelation 6:17

The question posed in this last verse of Revelation chapter 6 is, "Who is able to stand?" It is interesting that the Greek word for "be able to stand" is *du'ni mai* which also means power. The question then is, "Who will have the power to stand or survive the day of wrath?"

John begins to answer this question in Revelation chapter 7:

> [1]After these things I saw four angels standing at the four corners of the earth, holding the four winds of the earth,

that the wind should not blow on the earth, on the sea, or on any tree. [2]Then I saw another angel ascending from the east, having the seal of the living God. And he cried with a loud voice to the four angels to whom it was granted to harm the earth and the sea, [3]saying, "Do not harm the earth, the sea, or the trees till we have sealed the servants of our God on their foreheads." [4]And I heard the number of those who were sealed. One hundred and forty-four thousand of all the tribes of the children of Israel were sealed.   —Revelation 7:1-4

In this passage God commands the angels not to begin the judgments until they have sealed the servants of God on their foreheads. This sealing will protect God's people the same way Israel was protected in the land of Goshen during the last seven plagues that Moses pronounced over Egypt. It is the same protection against judgment that Noah and his family experienced as they were sealed. The rains of judgment did not fall until God had first sealed His people in the ark. The same will be true before the unfolding of the seventh seal, which is the great day of God's wrath.

Some cite this passage of Scripture as a proof text for a mid-trib rapture. They say that halfway through the seven-year tribulation period the church will be raptured. However, there are two major flaws with that interpretation. The first is that the tribulation period is only 3½ years in duration, not seven. This means something else has to take place the last 3½ years of the last week of this age. Of this fact, the Scriptures are clear. Immediately following the great tribulation or the fifth seal, the day of the Lord will be announced and carried out as depicted in the sixth and seventh seals. The second major flaw with this interpretation is that of mistaking the sealing of the servants of God as being synonymous with being raptured. If God's people were to be raptured off the earth, then there would be no need to protect them from the judgments being poured out upon the earth. For example, the locusts with the scorpion stings of the fifth trumpet are commanded to torment all mankind except those who have the seal of God on their foreheads. Since these locusts will not be released in heaven, one must assume that God is protecting His people who are still on this earth in their natural bodies.

The Number of Those Sealed

In Revelation 7:4-8, it says that the number sealed was 144,000 of all the tribes of the children of Israel. First let me say that I believe that John is writing parabolically here, not literally. Some teach that there will literally be 144,000 Jews saved and/or sealed before the opening of the seventh seal. Though this interpretation could satisfy what this Scripture says, it would violate what is clearly said in other Scriptures, such as Zechariah chapters 12 through 14. This passage of Scripture declares that Israel as a people will not acknowledge Jesus as their Messiah until His second coming. It says that Jerusalem will be surrounded by all the nations, half of the city will fall, and two-thirds of its inhabitants will be killed.

> [8]"And it shall come to pass in all the land," says the Lord, "That two-thirds in it shall be cut off and die, but one-third shall be left in it: [9]I will bring the one-third through the fire, will refine them as silver is refined, and test them as gold is tested. They will call on My name, and I will answer them. I will say, 'This is My people'; and each one will say, 'The Lord is my God.'"   —Zechariah 13:8-9

Just when it seems as though all hope is gone for the surviving Jewish remnant, Jesus will come again to this earth with His saints (the second coming) to reveal Himself as their Deliverer. When His feet touch down on the Mount of Olives, the mountain will cleave in two, forming a valley through which the surviving remnant will flee from the city to meet their Messiah. This remnant shall see Him whom they have pierced, and repent. They shall then join with the Lord and His saints to fight in the battle of Armageddon.

> ¹Behold, the day of the Lord is coming, and your spoil will be divided in your midst. ²For I will gather all the nations to battle against Jerusalem; the city shall be taken, the houses rifled, and the women ravished. Half of the city shall go into captivity, but the remnant of the people shall not be cut off from the city. ³Then the Lord will go forth and fight against those nations, as He fights in the day of battle. ⁴And in that day His feet will stand on the Mount of Olives, which faces Jerusalem on the east. And the Mount of Olives shall be split in two, from east to west, making a very large valley; half of the mountain shall move toward the north and half of it toward the south. ⁵Then you shall flee through My mountain valley, for the mountain valley shall reach to Azal ... Thus the Lord my God will come, and all the saints with You.
> —Zechariah 14:1-5

> ⁸In that day the Lord will defend the inhabitants of Jerusalem; the one who is feeble among them in that day shall be like David, and the house of David shall be like God, like the Angel of the Lord before them. ⁹It shall be in that day that I will seek to destroy all the nations that come against Jerusalem. ¹⁰"And I will pour on the house of David and on the inhabitants of Jerusalem the

Spirit of grace and supplication; then they will look on Me whom they pierced. Yes, they will mourn for Him as one mourns for his only son, and grieve for Him as one grieves for a firstborn. [11]In that day there shall be a great mourning in Jerusalem.   —Zechariah 12:8-11

This is a prophetic picture of what Paul was describing as the election of Israel in Romans chapters 9 and 11.

The Number Is Not Quantitative

The 144,000 who were sealed in Revelation chapter 7 was not about the quantity of those sealed but rather the quality (state of being) of those sealed. It is the same concept as seen in the number of the beast being 666. This is not speaking of the quantity of individuals that comprise the beast, but rather the quality or spiritual state of the beast. Often, God uses parabolic language to give greater insight and meaning to what He is describing. For instance, Jesus is not literally a lamb, but this descriptor is used to convey the truth that His innocent blood was shed in the same manner and for the same purpose as the passover lamb in Egypt. Another good example of the use of parabolic language can be seen in the various descriptors God uses when referencing the church. We know the church is not literally a field, a building, a city, a body, a woman, a man, or a mountain. Yet God has on occasion used these very descriptors and others to give greater understanding concerning the church's essence and function.

The Number Is Figurative

God often uses numbers symbolically in the Scriptures to convey deeper hidden meanings. After all, numbers are merely symbols man has created to represent quantities assigned to that which he encounters in life. However, the concepts and principles of life represented by these numbers were established by God. For example, the concept and principle of *one,* meaning the "only" of a kind, was conveyed by God. Man assigned the numeral *one* to represent this concept. God ascribes this principle to Himself, meaning He is the "only" of His kind. Marriage is another concept in which God uses numerical principles to convey a deeper hidden meaning to what is otherwise a very mysterious relationship. He describes it as the joining together of two "only's" into one "only." The numbers speak of quantities but concepts and principles are also conveyed that go far beyond the quantitative.

Though numbers are often used to express literal quantities, they can also be used typologically to express qualitative conditions and reoccurring patterns that God has ordained to be a part of His created order. Most Bible scholars agree the numeral "three" speaks figuratively of divine completeness and perfection; "seven" speaks figuratively of natural completeness and perfection; "ten" speaks of divine order as evidenced by the Ten Commandments. A divine pattern can also be seen by the fact that Noah was the tenth generation from Adam and Abraham was the tenth generation from Shem, the son of Noah. Was this just a coincidence or did God intend it to be more than that? God often uses numbers as both typological and qualitative illustrators. The Scriptures reveal concepts, principles, and patterns God has purposed to be an integral part of life. For us to ignore these would result in a shallowness of spiritual insight that could greatly limit our ability to understand and rightly relate to God.

I have written these several preceding paragraphs to introduce what I believe to be a deeper hidden meaning of the 144,000 taken from the twelve tribes of Israel. I am convinced that this number and this people group are figurative and are not meant to construe a quantitative head count of natural Jews. Let us now examine the typology of the nationality and the number – 144,000.

Let us look first at the national typology. Before doing so, I want to emphatically state that I am totally against "replacement theology." However, to deny that God uses the words "Israel" and "circumcision" to instruct the church in an exemplary and typological way would be foolishness. There is a natural Israel and a spiritual Israel of God. There is a natural circumcision and a spiritual circumcision depicted by God. All Jewish descendants are natural Jews, but not all natural Jews are spiritual Jews or the Israel of God. The true spiritual Jews in the eyes of God and the true spiritual Israel of God (Galatians 6:16) are those who are such inwardly, not outwardly. The true circumcision of God is one inwardly of the heart, not outwardly of the flesh. The following Scriptures should provide ample proof to support these declarations: Jeremiah 4:3-4, Romans 2:25-29, Romans 9:4-13, John 1:47-48, 1 Corinthians 10:18, Galatians 3:28-29, Galatians 4:24-26, Galatians 6:16, and Philippians 3:3. I am including several of these passages in the text below for the reader's convenience.

> 28For he is not a Jew who is one outwardly, nor is circumcision that which is outward in the flesh; 29but he is a Jew who is one inwardly; and circumcision is that of the heart, in the Spirit, not in the letter; whose praise is not from men but from God.   —Romans 2:28-29

> 47Jesus saw Nathanael coming toward Him, and said of him, "Behold, an Israelite indeed, in whom is no deceit!"   —John 1:47

¹⁶**And as many as walk according to this rule, peace and mercy be upon them, and upon the Israel of God.**

                                             —Galatians 6:16

³**For we are the circumcision, who worship God in the Spirit, rejoice in Christ Jesus, and have no confidence in the flesh.**   —Philippians 3:3

Most of these scriptural passages are addressing Gentile believers, confirming to them that they are a part of the Israel of God and the true circumcision.

And now let us look at the numeric typology. As God breaks down this number into groupings, you cannot help noticing the significance of the numeral "twelve." The 144,000 is divided into twelve groups of 12,000. "Twelve" is considered by many scholars to be a perfect number symbolizing God's power, authority, government, and lordship; it also speaks of completeness. The Bible contains many occurrences of the number twelve. As a matter of fact, it is found 187 times in the Scriptures. Other significant occurrences of the number twelve in the Scriptures would include the following: twelve months complete one year, twelve cakes of showbread on the table in the Holy Place, twelve tribes of Israel, twelve apostles, twelve spies, twelve fruits produced by the Tree of Life, and the twelve foundations and gates of the New Jerusalem.

The 144,000 is indicative of a perfect square (12x12) times a perfect cube (10x10x10), which could be figurative for a people in whom God's lordship has been divinely ordered. Some might say this conclusion is a little too far-fetched. However, would it be any more of a stretch of one's imagination to look at the biblical description of the New Jerusalem and conclude that this is speaking of the church, the Lamb's wife? Revelation chapter 21 clearly makes this conclusion for us without leaving it to the imagination of the reader. The dimensions, numbers, and descriptors of the New Jerusalem are intended to go far beyond a literal, quantitative interpretation.

> [2]Then I, John, saw the holy city, New Jerusalem, coming down out of heaven from God, prepared as a bride adorned for her husband.... [9]Then one of the seven angels who had the seven bowls filled with the seven last plagues came to me and talked with me, saying, "Come, I will show you the bride, the Lamb's wife." [10]And he carried me away in the Spirit to a great and high mountain, and showed me the great city, the holy Jerusalem, descending out of heaven from God.　　　—Revelation 21:2,9-10

The New Jerusalem represents a perfect cube (12,000 furlongs long x 12,000 furlongs wide x 12,000 furlongs high). This is not a literal city but rather a figure of the church perfected and brought into complete maturity by God. It would be ludicrous to think that there would be a walled city on this earth whose actual dimensions are 1,500 miles long x 1,500 miles wide x 1,500 miles high. Keep in mind that it only takes 18 miles to exit the earth's atmosphere, which would mean this city would extend 1,482 miles into outer space. The language being used here is parabolic, not literal.

Who Are the 144,000?

It is important to note that the book of Revelation which John received was for the church, about the church, and to the church. Most of the parabolic language in this revelation is in reference to the church or some portion of the church. Some examples of that which I am speaking would include the seven lampstands of

Revelation chapter 1, the twenty-four elders of Revelation chapter 4, the 144,000 sealed in Revelation chapter 7, the great multitude of Revelation 7, the temple of Revelation chapter 11, the woman and manchild of Revelation chapter 12, the firstfruits redeemed from those alive on the earth of Revelation chapter 14, the armies of Revelation chapter 19, and the New Jerusalem of Revelation chapter 21, which is the bride and wife of the Lamb of God.

Another group of 144,000 is found in Revelation 14:1. This is a different group than the one found in Revelation chapter 7. Revelation 7 represents a group of God's people who are sealed before the great day of God's wrath to protect them from the judgments that are about to unfold. Revelation chapter 14 represents a group of people who are redeemed from the earth as a firstfruits offering unto God before the tribulation period begins. These are not redeemed from the grave but from men who are alive on the earth.

Having said all of this, I still entertain the possibility that those being sealed in Revelation 7 could be the natural Israelites who one day shall be heirs of salvation. Since election is based on God's choosing before the foundations of the earth were laid, God would have to preserve from the judgment and death those chosen out of Israel to participate in the salvation of the Lord at His coming. However, my first choice is the church who overcame and survived the great tribulation.

Comparing Sign 7 with Seal 7

Sign 7:

We showed you from the Scriptures that the sixth sign immediately following the great tribulation is that the sun, moon, stars, and even the principalities and powers of the heavens will be shaken and affected. All the tribes of the earth will mourn when they see this sign because of the impending judgments that will soon follow.

Whereas the sixth sign is the announcement of coming judgments, the seventh sign is the actual outpouring of these judgments. Prior to this outpouring, God will send His angels to gather together His elect from the four corners of the world. His purpose is to identify, seal, and protect them from the coming judgments. The example of Noah is used to give us greater understanding of this event. Just as it was in the days of Noah, so shall it be in the coming of the day of the Lord. God gathered Noah and his family into the ark and sealed it before the rains came. He also uses the illustrations of two in a field and two grinding at a mill. One will be gathered unto the Lord and the other will be left outside of the protective covering of the Lord during the judgments.

Seal 7:

The seventh seal is the outpouring of seven trumpets or bowls of judgment on the earth and its inhabitants in the day of His wrath. It begins immediately after the saints are sealed, referring to the great multitude depicted in Revelation 7:9-17. These overcame during the great tribulation and washed their robes in the blood of the Lamb.

> [15]Therefore they are before the throne of God, and serve Him day and night in His temple. And He who sits on the throne will dwell among them. [16]They shall neither hunger anymore nor thirst anymore; the sun shall not strike them, nor any heat; [17]for the Lamb who is in the

midst of the throne will shepherd them and lead them to living fountains of waters. And God will wipe away every tear from their eyes.   —Revelation 7:15-17

During the great day of God's wrath, the Lamb of God will dwell among them and protect them from judgments such as hunger, thirst, being scorched by the sun or any heat. Jesus will shepherd these and lead them to living fountains of water while the rest of the world will be drinking the bitter red waters of judgment.

20

Same Story Told Twice
(part 1)

Introduction

Now that we have compared the seven seals with the Olivet Discourse, let us compare the same story told twice in the book of Revelation. The first comparison involved what Jesus taught from heaven with what Jesus taught on the earth concerning eschatology. Similarly, this next comparison involves the sharing of a story from a heavenly perspective with the same story told again from an earthly perspective.

Remember, the book of Revelation is divided into three sections. In Revelation 1:19 John is instructed to ""Write the things which you have seen, and the things which are, and the things which will take place after this." Note that "the things which are" related to the current condition of seven churches in Asia Minor in approximately 95 AD, and "the things which will take place after this" occur after 95 AD. The revelation he recorded after

Revelation 4:1 was an eschatological expose of things that were to occur after 95 AD.

> [1]After this I looked, and behold, a door standing open in heaven! And the first voice which I had heard addressing me like [the calling of] a war trumpet said, Come up here, and I will show you what must take place in the future.
> —Revelation 4:1 AMPC

Now let's look at the same story told twice which begins from a heavenly perspective in Revelation chapter 4 and finishes with Revelation chapter 12. It is told again from an earthly perspective beginning with Revelation chapter 13 through Revelation 20:6.

The Heavenly Story Begins

The story of the future begins in Revelation chapter 4 with a description of spiritual activities taking place in heaven. Since the first rendition of the story is as seen in heaven, its focus is from a heavenly, not earthly perspective. It describes God sitting on His throne in great glory and splendor. It depicts the twenty-four elders seated on thrones and the four living creatures worshipping Him who was seated upon the throne.

In Revelation chapter 5 we see a scroll with seven seals being held in the right hand of God. No man could be found in heaven that was worthy to open the scroll and loose its seals. However, one of the elders told John that the Lion of the tribe of Judah had prevailed to open the scroll and loose its seals. This worthy One, who was described as a Lamb who had been slain, came and took the scroll out of the hand of God and prepared to open the seals.

In Revelation chapter 6 we see the Lamb of God opening the first six of the seven seals. As we have shared previously, the first four seals occur before the beginning of the tribulation period, which is the fifth seal. It is during this fifth seal that all the saints of God will be persecuted and many martyred. The great tribulation will last 3½ years followed by another 3½ years of the great day of God's wrath. The saints will be sealed and protected before God's judgments are poured out upon all who dwell upon the face of the earth. This is recorded in the sixth and seventh seals.

As you might imagine, the amount of information concerning what is happening in heaven is far less than that which is happening on the earth, even though much of the heavenly activity is being directed upon the earth. Now let us look at what is happening on the earth during this same time period.

The Earthly Story Begins

The story of the future being told the second time begins in Revelation chapter 13 with a description of spiritual and natural activities taking place on the earth. Since the second rendition of the story is as seen on earth, its focus is primarily from an earthly, not heavenly, perspective. It describes the satanically-empowered beast rising up out of the sea of humanity. This beast had seven heads, ten horns, and ten crowns (7-10-10).

> ¹Then I stood on the sand of the sea. And I saw a beast rising up out of the sea, having seven heads and ten horns, and on his horns ten crowns, and on his heads a blasphemous name.   —Revelation 13:1

When it comes to solving the mystery of what the seven heads and ten horns of the beast represent, the interpretation is not left to the reader. God gave His own interpretation as to their meanings in Revelation chapter 17.

> [8]The beast that you saw was, and is not, and will ascend out of the bottomless pit and go to perdition. And those who dwell on the earth will marvel, whose names are not written in the Book of Life from the foundation of the world, when they see the beast that was, and is not, and yet is. [9]"Here is the mind which has wisdom: The seven heads are seven mountains on which the woman sits. [10]There are also seven kings. Five have fallen, one is, and the other has not yet come. And when he comes, he must continue a short time. [11]The beast that was, and is not, is himself also the eighth, and is of the seven, and is going to perdition. [12]The ten horns which you saw are ten kings who have received no kingdom as yet, but they receive authority for one hour as kings with the beast. [13]These are of one mind, and they will give their power and authority to the beast."   —Revelation 17:8-13

The seven heads are seven mountains (or empires) and their seven kings, who all play a significant role in the history and future of the nation of Israel. The ten horns are ten future kings that one day will receive power and authority to rule under and for the beast.

As we stated earlier in this book, the account in Revelation chapter 13 is an earlier depiction of the beast than the one found in Revelation chapter 12. The account in Revelation 12 depicts the dragon which empowers the beast of Revelation 13 as having seven heads, ten horns, and seven crowns (7-10-7). How do we know that the (7-10-10) version of the beast in Revelation 13 is an earlier version than the (7-10-7) version of Revelation 12? To answer that question, we need to look at the book of Daniel. As the beast described in Revelation 13 emerges and comes into power, there will be ten kingdoms and ten rulers over those kingdoms. However, another king will rise up amongst them and prevail against three of the ten rulers. Therefore, there will still be ten kingdoms (horns) but only seven rulers (crowns).

> 7"After this I saw in the night visions, and behold, a fourth beast, dreadful and terrible, exceedingly strong. It had huge iron teeth; it was devouring, breaking in pieces, and trampling the residue with its feet. It was different from all the beasts that were before it, and it had ten horns. 8I was considering the horns, and there was another horn, a little one, coming up among them, before whom three of the first horns were plucked out by the roots. And there, in this horn, were eyes like the eyes of a man, and a mouth speaking pompous words.   —Daniel 7:7-8

> 24The ten horns are ten kings who shall arise from this kingdom. And another shall rise after them; he shall be different from the first ones, and shall subdue three kings. 25He shall speak pompous words against the Most High, shall persecute the saints of the Most High, and shall intend to change times and laws. Then the saints shall be given into his hand for a time and times and half a time.
> —Daniel 7:24-25

This one who overthrows the other three kings is the Antichrist that was prophesied to come at the end of the age. This king arises after the original ten kings. I believe his beginnings are very insignificant and innocuous, and through peace, flattery, and deceit will become exceedingly strong with a small number of people, as stated in Daniel chapter 11. We share more insight on Antichrist in next subtopic.

Revelation 13:2 states that this beast will have traits like a leopard, a bear, and a lion. He will receive his power and great authority from Satan himself.

> ²Now the beast which I saw was like a leopard, his feet were like the feet of a bear, and his mouth like the mouth of a lion. The dragon gave him his power, his throne, and great authority.   —Revelation 13:2

This beast is described as being a composite of the first three beasts described in the vision found in Daniel 7.

> ²Daniel spoke, saying, "I saw in my vision by night, and behold, the four winds of heaven were stirring up the Great Sea. ³And four great beasts came up from the sea, each different from the other. ⁴The first was like a lion, and had eagle's wings. I watched till its wings were plucked off; and it was lifted up from the earth and made to stand on two feet like a man, and a man's heart was given to it. ⁵And suddenly another beast, a second, like a bear. It was raised up on one side, and had three ribs in its mouth between its teeth. And they said thus to it: 'Arise, devour much flesh!' ⁶After this I looked, and there was another, like a leopard, which had on its back four wings of a bird. The beast also had four heads, and dominion was given to it. ⁷After this I saw in the night visions, and behold, a fourth beast, dreadful and terrible, exceedingly strong. It had huge iron teeth; it was devouring, breaking in pieces, and trampling the residue with its feet. It was

different from all the beasts that were before it, and it had
ten horns."   —Daniel 7:2-7

As we look at the great image seen by Nebuchadnezzar in the
dream recorded in Daniel chapter 2, we learn of the last five kingdoms of the seven that make up the seven heads of the beast. The
last five empires in their chronological order are the Babylonians,
the Medes and Persians, the Greeks, the Romans, and the beast.
The Egyptian and Assyrian empires had already come and fallen
by the time of the reign of King Nebuchadnezzar to whom the
dream was given. One cannot help noticing the fact that there
is no other world empire between the fall of the Roman Empire
and the rise of the empire of the beast. However, there were notable dominant empires between these last two whose dominion
spanned significant portions of the world. The vision of Daniel
chapter 7 speaks of these when it describes the lion with the eagle's
wings, the bear, and the leopard with four heads and wings. The
first represents the United Kingdom, which was weakened when
the eagle's wings representing the United States were plucked from
her dominion. The bear is represented by the USSR (Union of
Soviet Socialist Republics). The leopard is represented by the Ger-
man Empire who in a span of thirty years seized dominion over
great portions of Europe and Africa on two different occasions. As
one compares the first three beasts with the fourth beast of Daniel
7:11-12, this passage seems to indicate that the first three beasts
were contemporaries of the fourth.

**¹¹"I watched then because of the sound of the pompous
words which the horn was speaking; I watched till the
beast was slain, and its body destroyed and given to the
burning flame. ¹²As for the rest of the beasts, they had**

their dominion taken away, yet their lives were prolonged
for a season and a time."   —Daniel 7:11-12

Daniel 7:23 also indicates that which makes the fourth beast
different from the other three beasts. It was that this one would
devour the whole world, tread it down, and break it in pieces.

23"Thus he said: 'The fourth beast shall be a fourth kingdom
on earth, which shall be different from all other kingdoms,
and shall devour the whole earth, trample it and break it in
pieces.'"   —Daniel 7:23

The Antichrist and His Mortal Wound

At the time of John's writing of this book, five of the seven
kings had already fallen. These five kings represented the world
empires of the Egyptians, Assyrians, Babylonians, Medes and Persians, and Greeks. The existing empire during John's life was the
Roman Empire. The king who was to come is the Antichrist who
becomes the ruler of the entire empire of the beast. He is described
as the king that was, and is not, and ascends out of the bottomless
pit. He will not only usurp authority over three of the ten kings
but will also assume the position as supreme leader over the entire
empire of the beast and its ten kingdoms. This Antichrist becomes
the eighth king but is also one of the original seven kings. Daniel
describes this king as one who is lightly esteemed and not one
who is honored in this final kingdom. It is also said of him that he
was a ruler of a small nation. How then could he attain to such a
prestigious position if that were the case? As we read the Scripture
passage that follows, this mystery begins to be revealed.

> [8]The beast that you saw was, and is not, and will ascend out of the bottomless pit and go to perdition. And those who dwell on the earth will marvel, whose names are not written in the Book of Life from the foundation of the world, when they see the beast that was, and is not, and yet is. [9]"Here is the mind which has wisdom: The seven heads are seven mountains on which the woman sits. [10]There are also seven kings. Five have fallen, one is, and the other has not yet come. And when he comes, he must continue a short time. [11]The beast that was, and is not, is himself also the eighth, and is of the seven, and is going to perdition."   —Revelation 17:8-11

This passage says that he was and is not, and at a future time he will ascend out of the bottomless pit. What does this mean? The phrase, "the beast that was," signifies that he did exist. The phrase, "is not," signifies that he stopped existing because he died. The phrase, "yet is," signifies that he who was dead exists again. How can this be? The answer is found in Revelation 13:3. In this verse John said he saw that one of the seven heads was mortally wounded but then was raised from the dead. As we shared earlier in Revelation chapter 17, this head or king was one of the seven heads that becomes the eighth. I believe that the seventh king who is yet to come will rule, but only for a short time, when most likely an assassination will take place. I personally believe that Satan will incarnate within his dead body, causing him to be raised from the dead. By so doing, Satan will have counterfeited the same story-line as the death and resurrection of Jesus Christ. There is nobody who should know better than Satan how effective that storyline was. Combine the beast's being raised from the dead with all the supernatural powers of Satan working through him, and it leaves little to the imagination as to why everyone marvels over him and worships him and the dragon. All whose names are not written in the Lamb's Book of Life will indeed worship him.

Whether or not this head, the seventh king, was wounded unto death and raised from the dead or his death/resurrection were counterfeited cannot be substantiated from the Scriptures. However, in the eyes of the world it obviously is received to be a genuine resurrection. Most will see him as being invincible and that none would be victorious who would wage war against him.

He receives authority to rule all the people and nations of the world for forty-two months. During his reign, he will blaspheme God, His name, His tabernacle, and all that dwell in heaven. It will be given unto him to make war against the saints of God and overcome them. This period of 42 months is known as the great tribulation period, during which time many saints will be martyred for their unwavering faith in the name of Jesus. Nominal and genuine Christians will both be tested during this time, but only those who endure to the end will be saved.

The False Prophet

During the great tribulation, another beast will arise out of the earth who will cause all who dwell on the earth to worship the first beast (Antichrist) whose deadly wound was healed. He will be able to do great wonders in the sight of men, such as calling fire down from heaven unto the earth. By means of extraordinary miracles he will be able to deceive all whose names are not written in the Book of Life. He will command that an image be made of the beast that was mortally wounded by the sword and did live. He has power to give life unto the image of the beast and even cause the image to speak. This image will actually have the authority to cause all who do not worship the image of the beast to be killed.

This second beast is referred to as the false prophet in Revelation 16:13; 19:20; and 20:10. He will exercise all the authority of the first beast and will institute a financial system where no one can buy or sell except they receive the mark of the beast in their right hand or in their foreheads. The story of the rise and rule of the false prophet can be seen in Revelation 13:9-18. I include this very important passage here for your convenience:

> [9]If anyone is able to hear, let him listen:
>
> [10]Whoever leads into captivity will himself go into captivity; if anyone slays with the sword, with the sword must he be slain. Herein is [the call for] the patience and the faith and fidelity of the saints (God's people). [11]Then I saw another beast rising up out of the land [itself]; he had two horns like a lamb, and he spoke (roared) like a dragon. [12]He exerts all the power and right of control of the former beast in his presence, and causes the earth and those who dwell upon it to exalt and deify the first beast, whose deadly wound was healed, and to worship him. [13]He performs great signs (startling miracles), even making fire fall from the sky to the earth in men's sight. [14]And because of the signs (miracles) which he is allowed to perform in the presence of the [first] beast, he deceives those who inhabit the earth, commanding them to erect a statue (an image) in the likeness of the beast who was wounded by the [small] sword and still lived. [15]And he is permitted [also] to impart the breath of life into the beast's image, so that the statue of the beast could actually talk and cause to be put to death those who would not bow down and worship the image of the beast. [16]Also

he compels all [alike], both small and great, both the rich and the poor, both free and slave, to be marked with an inscription [stamped] on their right hands or on their foreheads, [17]So that no one will have power to buy or sell unless he bears the stamp (mark, inscription), [that is] the name of the beast or the number of his name. [18]Here is [room for] discernment [a call for the wisdom of interpretation]. Let anyone who has intelligence (penetration and insight enough) calculate the number of the beast, for it is a human number [the number of a certain man]; his number is 666.   —Revelation 13:9-18 AMPC

Back and Forth

As we continue this study, we will go back and forth between the story being told from a heavenly perspective and the story being told from an earthly perspective. Using smaller portions of each perspective at a time will facilitate the process of comparing them point by point, event by event, or time period by time period. Keep in mind that the appearance of each point and event may seem to differ though they are speaking of the same thing. This is not because the point being made, the event, or the time period is different, but rather because the perspective from which they are being viewed is different.

21

Same Story Told Twice
(part 2)

Rejoining the Heavenly View

Now I would like to cover the events and time period up to but excluding the tribulation period.

As we rejoin the heavenly perspective, let us keep in mind that the first four seals of Revelation chapter 6 are all precursors of the great tribulation, which is the fifth seal. We will not give time nor space to the first four seals as we have covered these previously. However, if your memory is anything like mine, you might want to review these seals with their Olivet Discourse counterparts in chapters 15 and 16 of this book.

Now let us look at Revelation chapters 10 and 11. These chapters contain additional information not previously mentioned concerning this same time period.

Revelation 10

Let us also keep in mind that when reading these perspectives, one cannot read the book of Revelation chronologically. A classic example of this is seen as we begin reading Revelation chapter 10.

I personally believe that Revelation chapter 10 is a repeat of the same events and time period described in Revelation chapters 4 and 5. Let us take a moment to compare these passages.

Revelation 10 opens with a description of a mighty angel clothed with a cloud. A rainbow was on his head, his face was like the sun, and his feet were like pillars of fire.

> ¹I saw still another mighty angel coming down from heaven, clothed with a cloud. And a rainbow was on his head, his face was like the sun, and his feet like pillars of fire.
> —Revelation 10:1

Revelation chapter 4 seems to indicate that the one seated on the throne (Christ) is the same figure being spoken of as the mighty angel in Revelation chapter 10. Both had a rainbow over them and did shine brilliantly. The feet like pillars of fire remind me of the feet of the one like the Son of Man who stood in the midst of the candlesticks in Revelation chapter 1. There were also lightnings, thunders, and voices proceeding from the throne.

> ²Immediately I was in the Spirit; and behold, a throne set in heaven, and One sat on the throne. ³And He who sat there was like a jasper and a sardius stone in appearance; and there was a rainbow around the throne, in appearance like an emerald.
> —Revelation 4:2-3

Revelation chapter 10 also says that the angel had a little book in his hand. This same angel, having put his right foot on the sea and his left foot on the land, cried with a loud voice, as when a lion roars. When he cried out, seven thunders uttered their voices. John said that as he was about to write what he was seeing and hearing, a voice came from heaven saying, "Seal up the things which the seven thunders uttered, and do not write them."

> [2]He had a little book open in his hand. And he set his right foot on the sea and his left foot on the land, [3]and cried with a loud voice, as when a lion roars. When he cried out, seven thunders uttered their voices. [4]Now when the seven thunders uttered their voices, I was about to write; but I heard a voice from heaven saying to me, "Seal up the things which the seven thunders uttered, and do not write them."   —Revelation 10:2-4

Could this little book be the same scroll that was in the right hand of Him who sat upon the throne in Revelation chapter 5? Could the voice of a lion roaring be coming from the Lion of the tribe of Judah in Revelation 5? Could the seven thunders that uttered their voices be the thunderings in Revelation 4?

> [1]And I saw in the right hand of Him who sat on the throne a scroll written inside and on the back, sealed with seven seals. [2]Then I saw a strong angel proclaiming with a loud voice, "Who is worthy to open the scroll and to loose its seals?" [3]And no one in heaven or on the earth or under the earth was able to open the scroll, or to look at it.
>
> [4]So I wept much, because no one was found worthy to open and read the scroll, or to look at it. [5]But one of the elders said to me, "Do not weep. Behold, the Lion of the tribe of Judah, the Root of David, has prevailed to open the scroll and to loose its seven seals."
>   —Revelation 5:1-5

> [5]And from the throne proceeded lightnings, thunderings, and voices. Seven lamps of fire were burning before the throne, which are the seven Spirits of God.
>
> —Revelation 4:5

Now that we have shown the similarities between these two passages of Scripture, let us also look at one major difference. In Revelation chapters 4 and 5, the command went forth to unseal what was written. In Revelation chapter 10, the command went forth to seal up what was written. When I inquired of the Lord as to what this was about, a spontaneous thought immediately came to me that I personally believe was an answer from the Lord. It is yours to bear witness to, whether or not this was truly an answer from God. I felt like the Lord said, "The seven thunders were to be the complement to the seven seals like the seven bowls were to the seven trumpets. My next question was, "Lord, if this is true, why then do not the seven thunders and seven seals appear in opposite perspectives like the trumpets and bowls?" I continued to reason that the seven bowls are described in the earthly perspective of the story whereas the seven trumpets are described in the heavenly perspective. The one was in earthly language and the other in heavenly language, which needed to be interpreted to be understood on the earth. He said: "What is being shown and spoken in heaven cannot be seen or understood on earth unless someone is given access to heaven to be a witness of what he encountered." Without an open heaven available to someone, we would be totally clueless as to its happenings. Again I sensed the Lord speaking, "I purposely instructed John to seal up what he saw and heard so that the heavenly perspective would remain unknown on the earth." Since he did not relate what he saw and heard, the seven thunders remain an unintelligible mystery on the earth. This is why the seven thunders are seen in the heavenly perspective with its complement, the seven seals. I believe one day near the end of the age, God will unveil what the seven thunders uttered, that it might be understood from an earthly perspective. However, until that time comes they will remain concealed in the heavenly rendition of the story.

Before concluding Revelation chapter 10, I want to direct your attention to verses 8 through 11.

> **⁸Then the voice which I heard from heaven spoke to me again and said, "Go, take the little book which is open in the hand of the angel who stands on the sea and on the earth." ⁹So I went to the angel and said to him, "Give me the little book." And he said to me, "Take and eat it; and it will make your stomach bitter, but it will be as sweet as honey in your mouth." ¹⁰Then I took the little book out of the angel's hand and ate it, and it was as sweet as honey in my mouth. But when I had eaten it, my stomach became bitter. ¹¹And he said to me, "You must prophesy again about many peoples, nations, tongues, and kings."**
> **—Revelation 10:8-11**

In this passage John was told to take the book and eat it. It would be sweet like honey in his mouth but bitter in his stomach. Though the details of the seven thunders were to be kept a mystery, God did not want to hide the fact that the overall effect of them would be very bitter or negative. Then in verse 11 above, God makes a very interesting statement to John, saying, "You must prophesy again..." This presumes that he has already prophesied the story once and was being asked to do it again. Could this be yet another proof text that the same story is to be told or prophesied twice? It is also interesting to note that he was to prophesy again not to the nation of Israel, as some suggest, but to many peoples, nations, tongues, and kings. I reiterate, "This book is not about Israel, for Israel, or to Israel."

Revelation 11

In Revelation chapter 11, the first two verses are the only ones which relate to this same time period ramping up to the tribulation period.

> ¹Then I was given a reed like a measuring rod. And the angel stood, saying, "Rise and measure the temple of God, the altar, and those who worship there. ²But leave out the court which is outside the temple, and do not measure it, for it has been given to the Gentiles. And they will tread the holy city underfoot for forty-two months."
>
> —Revelation 11:1-2

These two verses depict a measuring of the temple of God. First of all we must specify what this temple is that is referred to in verse one. Is this a rebuilt temple in Jerusalem near the end of the age? If so, what are God's people doing worshipping in this temple? Only Jewish priests would be allowed to worship in that temple. No, the New Testament is very clear as to what God considers His temple to be, following the death of Jesus Christ. The Scriptures specifically define the temple of God as one made without the hands of man. The individual Christian and the corporate church are clearly stated to be the temple of God in 1 Corinthians 6:19-20 and 3:16-17 respectively. God has no intention of inhabiting a temple made with hands in the remainder of this age.

Notice that not only was John to measure the temple of God but also the golden altar and those who worship there. This measurement is a spiritual judgment which looks not at the outward appearance but looks inwardly at the hearts of those being measured. See 1 Samuel 16:7 and John 7:24. Dear Christian, if you are the temple of God, then you have an outer court, a holy place, and a most holy place. The outer court Christians are those who primarily walk by natural light, whereas inner court Christians are those who have learned to go into the inner recesses of their beings to worship God in spirit and truth. God specifically wanted John to separate His people into two different groups ... those who worship externally and those true worshippers who worship God internally. The external, outer court Christians will be given to the world to be tribulated 42 months (3½ years). I believe those who are measured to be the true worshippers are those who used the things they willingly suffered to mature into the overcoming believers as represented by the manchild of Revelation chapter 12.

Rejoining the Earthly View

As we rejoin the earthly perspective, let us focus on the same time period spoken of in the first four seals of Revelation chapter 6. To do this, we will be looking at portions of Revelation chapters 13 and 14. Our focus will be to compare the second telling of the same story with the first.

Revelation 13

Though we covered Revelation chapter 13 in the previous chapter of this book, I want us to take another look specifically to that which pertains to the time frame we are now studying. The beast that rises up out of the sea does so before the tribulation of the fifth seal occurs. The Antichrist, who usurps power over three of the ten kings and who was healed of his deadly wound, also comes forth before the fifth seal. We can conclude this from the heavenly rendition of this story in Revelation chapter 12. In this passage the great red dragon, who is waiting to devour the manchild as soon as he is born, has seven heads, ten horns, and only seven crowns. This substantiates the fact that the power grab of the Antichrist occurs prior to the catching up of the firstfruits manchild and the subsequent tribulation of the church who birthed him.

Revelation 14

Revelation chapter 14 begins with the mention of another group of 144,000 saints. This is not the same group of 144,000 spoken of in Revelation chapter 7. Remember, that group was sealed by the Holy Spirit after the great tribulation and just prior to the great day of God's wrath.

> ¹Then I looked, and behold, a Lamb standing on Mount Zion, and with Him one hundred and forty-four thousand, having His Father's name written on their foreheads. ²And I heard a voice from heaven, like the voice of many waters, and like the voice of loud thunder. And I heard the sound of harpists playing their harps. ³They sang as it were a new song before the throne, before the four living creatures, and the elders; and no one could learn that song except the hundred and forty-four thousand who were redeemed from the earth.
>
> —Revelation 14:1-3

Who are they and who is their counterpart in the first telling of the same story? Whoever they are, there is no mention of any literal or figurative identification with Israel. These are standing on Mount Zion (figurative speech for the church) with the Lamb, and they have His Father's name written on their foreheads. Remember, at this time the Jews have not yet received Jesus to be their Messiah and therefore are not the children of God. That does not happen until the second coming of Christ to this earth. These are not Jews. Neither do these represent all of the Christians at that point in time. These are described as those who were redeemed from the earth from amongst men. They were redeemed from the living, not from the grave, which means this could not be referring to the rapture of the entire church. No, these are just the firstfruits redeemed unto God and to the Lamb from those who are alive on the earth.

Their counterpart in the first telling of the story is the overcoming manchild company of Revelation chapter 12. These are they who are the true internal worshippers who through intimacy have come to know the Lamb and are led by His Spirit to follow Him wherever He goes. These are described as virgins who refuse to give themselves to anyone other than the Lamb of God. There is no deceit in their mouth and they come faultless inside the temple to worship before His throne. These are truly the ones measured by John in Revelation 11:1-2 who worship within at the golden altar prior to the unfolding of the 42 months of great tribulation.

22

Same Story Told Twice
(part 3)

Rejoining the Heavenly View

Again let us rejoin the heavenly perspective. Here we want to discuss the time period represented by the great tribulation. The first reference to this period from the heavenly perspective is seen in the fifth seal of Revelation chapter 6:

> [9]When He opened the fifth seal, I saw under the altar the souls of those who had been slain for the word of God and for the testimony which they held. [10]And they cried with a loud voice, saying, "How long, O Lord, holy and true, until You judge and avenge our blood on those who dwell on the earth?" [11]Then a white robe was given to each of them; and it was said to them that they should rest a little while longer, until both the number of their fellow servants and their brethren, who would be killed as they were, was completed.   —Revelation 6:9-11

This Scripture not only talks about the martyred saints throughout the past but also about those who would be martyred by the beast and his government. For your convenience, you can review what we have already covered concerning this seal in chapter 17 of this book. Now let us look at other Scriptures that discuss this event in the first telling of the story.

Revelation 12

As we learned in our earlier study of Revelation chapter 12, the woman is representative of the church, travailing to give birth to the overcoming manchild company that is currently being formed in her midst. The coming birth marks a time of separating the two, like that described in the measuring of the temple of God in Revelation chapter 11. This separation is not one of spiritual identity but rather of spiritual state of being. The mature overcoming believers will be caught up unto God before the tribulation period begins. These will be counted worthy to escape the coming events because they had been faithful to watch unto prayer in the holy place (see Luke 21:36 and Revelation 3:10). These who are ready and watching will be offered up unto God as a firstfruits offering of the coming main harvest or rapture of the church.

> [36]"Watch therefore, and pray always that you may be counted worthy to escape all these things that will come to pass, and to stand before the Son of Man.   —Luke 21:36

> [10]Because you have kept My command to persevere, I also will keep you from the hour of trial which shall come upon the whole world, to test those who dwell on the earth.   —Revelation 3:10

This event will precipitate the woman's fleeing into the wilderness where she will be persecuted by the great red dragon for 1,260 days.

> [5]She bore a male Child who was to rule all nations with a rod of iron. And her Child was caught up to God and His throne. [6]Then the woman fled into the wilderness, where she has a place prepared by God, that they should feed her there one thousand two hundred and sixty days.... [13]Now when the dragon saw that he had been cast to the earth, he persecuted the woman who gave birth to the male Child.   —Revelation 12:5-6, 13

God's involvement in this is clear. The Scripture says that God will prepare a place for His church in this wilderness testing. This place is a table of provision set by the Great Shepherd for all of His flock who are walking into or through the valley of the shadow of death. It is in this valley that they shall learn to trust in God as their provider and learn to become true internal worshippers of God.

> [14]But the woman was given two wings of a great eagle, that she might fly into the wilderness to her place, where she is nourished for a time and times and half a time, from the presence of the serpent. [15]So the serpent spewed water out of his mouth like a flood after the woman, that he might cause her to be carried away by the flood. [16]But the earth helped the woman, and the earth opened its mouth and swallowed up the flood which the dragon had spewed out of his mouth.   —Revelation 12:14-16

This provision of God for their daily life will continue, extending beyond their 3½ years of wilderness testing. These will be sealed and kept from the judgments of the day of the Lord that will come to judge all those who dwell on earth.

[13]Then one of the elders answered, saying to me, "Who are these arrayed in white robes, and where did they come from?" [14]And I said to him, "Sir, you know." So he said to me, "These are the ones who come out of the great tribulation, and washed their robes and made them white in the blood of the Lamb. [15]Therefore they are before the throne of God, and serve Him day and night in His temple. And He who sits on the throne will dwell among them. [16]They shall neither hunger anymore nor thirst anymore; the sun shall not strike them, nor any heat; [17]for the Lamb who is in the midst of the throne will shepherd them and lead them to living fountains of waters. And God will wipe away every tear from their eyes."   —Revelation 7:13-17

I am convinced that the group of saints being described here are not those who were martyred during the great tribulation. Those saints are already enjoying the perfect peace and pleasures of the Lord in heaven where there is no lack of any good thing. However, these are they who endured the wilderness testing to the end. Because of their endurance, they will have access to God's presence in His temple daily. God will dwell among them. Even in the midst of the severely deteriorating conditions of a world suffering from the judgments of God, they will enjoy God's supernatural provision. God will feed them and give them drink. He will protect them from the sun and heat that will be tormenting those who dwell on the earth. He shall shepherd them and lead them to living fountains of waters while the inhabitants of the earth are drinking the bloody, bitter waters of judgment. He will wipe away every tear of sorrow while the world bitterly weeps.

Though the devil means this time of tribulation for bad, God has purposed it for good. He will use this time for the express purpose of maturing His people spiritually through the things they suffer, even as it was so with their Lord.

> [10]For it was fitting for Him, for whom are all things and by whom are all things, in bringing many sons to glory, to make the captain of their salvation perfect through sufferings.   —Hebrews 2:10

> [7]...who, in the days of His flesh, when He had offered up prayers and supplications, with vehement cries and tears to Him who was able to save Him from death, and was heard because of His godly fear, [8]though He was a Son, yet He learned obedience by the things which He suffered.   —Hebrews 5:7-8

It will be given unto those who are martyred or endure to the end of this 3½ year process to overcome by the blood of the Lamb and by the word of their testimony.

Rejoining the Earthly View

The only place the tribulation period is referenced in the earthly view is in a few verses in Revelation chapters 13 and 14.

Revelation 13

Revelation chapter 13 looks at this time period through the lens of the beast, or Antichrist, and the false prophet. We know that the beast is given power to continue in his reign for 42 months.

> [5]And he was given a mouth speaking great things and blasphemies, and he was given authority to continue for forty-two months.   —Revelation 13:5

Never lose sight of the fact that all authority, and those who exercise it, is delegated by God. He alone determines who, where, and how long one rules.

> ¹Let every soul be subject to the governing authorities. For there is no authority except from God, and the authorities that exist are appointed by God.
> —Romans 13:1

The first reference to the tribulation of the saints is this:

> ⁶Then he opened his mouth in blasphemy against God, to blaspheme His name, His tabernacle, and those who dwell in heaven. ⁷It was granted to him to make war with the saints and to overcome them. And authority was given him over every tribe, tongue, and nation.
> —Revelation 13:6-7

We know from our previous studies that the Antichrist will persecute and prevail against the saints of God for 42 months. This 42 month (3½ year) period is called the great tribulation. In Revelation 13:10, it says, "Here is the patience and faith of the saints." The word for "patience" in the Greek is *hypomone* and means "enduring, sustaining perseverance under misfortunes and trials." Part of the misfortunes and trials will be that if one does not worship the beast and the image of the beast, they will be killed. Also one must swear allegiance to and receive the mark of the beast or they will not be able to buy or sell (Revelation 13:15-17).

Revelation 14

In Revelation chapter 14, we see through a lens that is focused on the firstfruits overcomers. This chapter begins talking about the manchild, who is the firstfruits offering to God and to the Lamb. We know from our previous studies that as soon as the manchild is caught up unto God, the woman (who is the church) flees into the wilderness where she is persecuted. Revelation 14:6 says that the everlasting gospel will be preached unto them that dwell on the earth. In comparing this verse with the Olivet Discourse in Matthew 24, we know that this event happens during the great tribulation.

> [6]Then I saw another angel flying in the midst of heaven, having the everlasting gospel to preach to those who dwell on the earth – to every nation, tribe, tongue, and people.   —Revelation 14:6

> [13]But he who endures to the end shall be saved. [14]And this gospel of the kingdom will be preached in all the world as a witness to all the nations, and then the end will come.
> —Matthew 24:13-14

Revelation 14:12-13 also refers to the saints in tribulation. It speaks again about the patient endurance of the saints and the blessing some will receive through martyrdom.

> [12]Here is the patience of the saints; here are those who keep the commandments of God and the faith of Jesus. [13]Then I heard a voice from heaven saying to me, "Write: 'Blessed are the dead who die in the Lord from now on.'"   —Revelation 14:12-13

23

Same Story Told Twice
(part 4)

Rejoining the Heavenly View

Now let's compare the day of the Lord from the two perspectives. To do this, we will be comparing the sixth and seventh seals with their counterparts as seen from an earthly perspective in Revelation chapters 14 through 16.

The Sixth Seal

The day of the Lord, also known as the great day of the wrath of the Lamb, is depicted in the sixth and seventh seals. The sixth seal takes place immediately after the days of tribulation of the fifth seal. This is what Jesus taught on earth and is what He has also taught from heaven. The events of this seal are basically the signs in the heavens, the announcement of the coming of God's wrath, man's reactions to the announcement, and the sealing of the saints who are not appointed to the wrath.

¹²I looked when He opened the sixth seal, and behold, there was a great earthquake; and the sun became black as sackcloth of hair, and the moon became like blood. ¹³And the stars of heaven fell to the earth, as a fig tree drops its late figs when it is shaken by a mighty wind. ¹⁴Then the sky receded as a scroll when it is rolled up, and every mountain and island was moved out of its place. ¹⁵And the kings of the earth, the great men, the rich men, the commanders, the mighty men, every slave and every free man, hid themselves in the caves and in the rocks of the mountains, ¹⁶and said to the mountains and rocks, "Fall on us and hide us from the face of Him who sits on the throne and from the wrath of the Lamb! ¹⁷For the great day of His wrath has come, and who is able to stand?"

—Revelation 6:12-17

We have already compared this seal with its counterpart sign in the Olivet Discourse in chapters 18 and 19 of this book. In both instances, the sun is darkened, the moon is turned blood red, and heavenly debris falls to the earth in appearance as shooting stars. One thing is for sure. It will be a terrifying time for those who are appointed unto God's wrath and a very sobering one for those who are not. I believe it is high time that the church begins to diligently prepare for this coming of the Lord and, like Noah, unashamedly warn everybody we can of the impending judgment.

Seventh Seal/the Prelude to Seven Trumpets

Whereas the sixth seal was the announcement of the day of the Lord's wrath, the seventh seal is the actual pouring out of the judgments of God to punish the wickedness of sinners. This seventh seal is composed of seven trumpets, which will be blown to signal seven specific judgments that will severely affect planet earth and those who dwell upon it during the day of the Lord.

> [1]When He opened the seventh seal, there was silence in heaven for about half an hour. [2]And I saw the seven angels who stand before God, and to them were given seven trumpets. [3]Then another angel, having a golden censer, came and stood at the altar. He was given much incense, that he should offer it with the prayers of all the saints upon the golden altar, which was before the throne. [4]And the smoke of the incense, with the prayers of the saints, ascended before God from the angel's hand. [5]Then the angel took the censer, filled it with fire from the altar, and threw it to the earth. And there were noises, thunderings, lightnings, and an earthquake. [6]So the seven angels who had the seven trumpets prepared themselves to sound.
>
> —Revelation 8:1-6

Rejoining the Earthly View

There is very little covered from the earthly view concerning the sixth seal. Of the major events of the sixth seal, only the sealing of the saints is recorded in the earthly perspective.

Reaping the Ripe Grapes of God (the Elect):

> [14]Then I looked, and behold, a white cloud, and on the cloud sat One like the Son of Man, having on His head a golden crown, and in His hand a sharp sickle. [15]And another angel came out of the temple, crying with a loud voice to Him who sat on the cloud, "Thrust in Your sickle and reap, for the time has come for You to reap, for the harvest of the earth is ripe." [16]So He who sat on the

cloud thrust in His sickle on the earth, and the earth was
reaped.   —Revelation 14:14-16

This is the first of two reapings in this passage of Scripture.
The first one shown here is the gathering of the elect of God from
the whole earth as seen in Matthew 24:31. It is the same event as
the sealing of the 144,000 in Revelation 7:1-8.

Reaping the Grapes of Wrath (the Wicked):

[17]Then another angel came out of the temple which is
in heaven, he also having a sharp sickle. [18]And another
angel came out from the altar, who had power over fire,
and he cried with a loud cry to him who had the sharp
sickle, saying, "Thrust in your sharp sickle and gather the
clusters of the vine of the earth, for her grapes are fully
ripe." [19]So the angel thrust his sickle into the earth and
gathered the vine of the earth, and threw it into the great
winepress of the wrath of God.   —Revelation 14:17-19

This second reaping is the gathering of the ungodly, who willingly received the mark of the beast, to be cast into the great winepress of the wrath of God. The ones reaped here are those who
receive the judgments of the seventh seal and its seven trumpets/
bowls. To see what Revelation 14:19 describes as "the great winepress of the wrath of God" is like, we must look at the seven bowls
of judgment that follow in Revelation chapters 15 and 16. We will
now look at this great event by comparing the heavenly perspective
(the seven trumpets) with the earthly perspective (the seven bowls).

Before beginning this comparison, however, we want to examine some biblical details as seen and perceived from the heavenly
perspective, which is the weightier of the two perspectives. Not

everything that is seen from an earthly vantage point is as it seems. Though both perspectives can be seen from the heavenly perspective, the earthly perspective is limited to natural manifestations. Generally speaking, the spiritual activities that influence and cause these things to happen in the natural often go unseen by the natural senses. There are some details seen in the trumpets that are not evident in the bowls. The trumpets are divided into two groups. The first four trumpets represent one group and the last three another.

The first four trumpets bring devastation primarily to the world in which man lives. The last three are aimed more directly at man, though mankind is affected and hurt by all the trumpets. This is significant since these first four affect areas that God created to provide a blessed environment for man's existence. The four areas affected – the earth, sea, fresh water, and sky – made up the whole of the human environment as the ancients perceived it. Another detail also noted in the first four trumpets is that one-third of each target area will be affected by these judgments. What is God trying to tell us about the repetitive use of "one-third"? Is it possible that it has to do with God's generosity? God destroys one-third but spares two-thirds. The limitation to "one-third but spares two-thirds" also leaves room for more terrible destruction to come. The previous judgments of the fourth seal caused one-fourth of mankind to die, which is less than the one-third affected later in the first four trumpets. It is apparent that God intensifies the severity of judgments when men ignore the warnings of earlier judgments. The first four trumpets seem to serve not only as judgments but also as warnings of the last three trumpets, since they are far worse.

The last three trumpets, when viewed from a heavenly perspective, cause an angel to fly through heaven proclaiming with a loud voice an ominous warning because of the severity of the three trumpets that are yet to sound. His exact words were, "Woe, woe, woe to the inhabitants of the earth, because of the other voices of the trumpet of the three angels, which are yet to sound!" (Rev. 8:13) These are often referred to by Bible scholars as the "three woes" of the great day of God's wrath.

Historic Examples of Galactic Judgments

In three of the first four trumpets, we see some type of heavenly mass fall from the heavens, through the atmosphere, and striking some portion of planet earth. When the Bible makes reference to stars falling from heaven and hitting the earth, it cannot be talking about literal stars. Most stars are much greater in size than the earth and thereby would require only one to completely obliterate our planet. When people point out shooting stars streaking through the night sky, these are obviously not stars but rather debris from outer space entering earth's atmosphere. I believe the judgments of these first three trumpets are a result of meteors and asteroids of varying sizes being broken up in the atmosphere and falling to the earth. These asteroids are masses of rock which vary in size from just a few miles to several hundred. About 3,500 asteroids have been cataloged, and more are discovered each year.

According to studies conducted at the University of California, an asteroid of this magnitude would be so hot by the time it hit an ocean that it would make a large part of the ocean water anoxic (oxygen deficient) by simply boiling the oxygen out of that area of the sea. Sea temperatures would rise dramatically and hot water would kill billions of sea creatures in a very large radius. The warmed anoxic water resulting from the impact would also provide a perfect environment for the growth of red algae or what is known as red tide.

When John said the sea turned to blood, he may have been describing the appearance of red algae, which thrives in oxygen-deficient water! Can you imagine what massive tidal waves would result from debris this size striking our seas in numerous places?

History provides us with some historic examples of the coming attractions God prophesies as judgments on this earth in the last days. One such example is a single meteorite which fell in Siberia in 1908, devastating over 1,000 square miles. The shock was felt as far away as Europe, while trees up to 20 miles away were blown down. Yet the 1908 meteorite was only about 200 feet across – a far cry from one mile across or greater!

Comparing the First Four Trumpets/Bowls

The First Trumpet

Let us now examine the specifics of the first trumpet. When looking at the trumpets and bowls, we want to particularly focus on their target areas or the areas being affected by their judgments. In the case of the first trumpet, the target area is the *earth* or the "dry land" as Genesis 1:9-10 describes it. Hail and fire, mingled with blood, will be thrown to the earth. This will cause one-third of all the trees and green grass to be burned up.

> ⁷The first angel sounded: And hail and fire followed, mingled with blood, and they were thrown to the earth. And a third of the trees were burned up, and all green grass was burned up.   —Revelation 8:7

The First Bowl

In the case of the first bowl, the target area is the *earth*. Notice the target area of both the trumpet and the bowl are the same. Remember, any difference seen between the trumpet and bowl, as we have explained previously, is due to their being seen from different perspectives (heavenly or earthly). Therefore, it is important to add together all the parts to get a composite picture of what will really transpire. From the bowl we learn additional information as to how that which happens in the first trumpet affects more than the green vegetation of the earth. It also causes a foul and loathsome sore to come upon all who received the mark of the beast and worshiped his image.

> ²So the first went and poured out his bowl upon the earth, and a foul and loathsome sore came upon the men who had the mark of the beast and those who worshiped his image.   —Revelation 16:2

The Second Trumpet

In the case of the second trumpet, the target area is the *sea*. A great mountain burning with fire was thrown into the sea. This could be the result of a large meteor shower or an asteroid striking the sea. This will cause one-third of the sea to become blood, resulting in the death of one-third of the living creatures in the sea and the destruction of one-third of the ships on the sea.

> ⁸Then the second angel sounded: And something like a great mountain burning with fire was thrown into the sea, and a third of the sea became blood. ⁹And a third of the living creatures in the sea died, and a third of the ships were destroyed.   —Revelation 8:8-9

The Second Bowl

In the case of the second bowl, the target area is the *sea*. Again you will notice that the target area of both the second trumpet and second bowl is the same. In the earthly view, the only difference is the exclusion of the one-third of the ships being destroyed as described in the heavenly view. Remember, to get a more complete picture of what will take place we must look at a composite of the two perspectives.

> ³Then the second angel poured out his bowl on the sea, and it became blood as of a dead man; and every living creature in the sea died.   —Revelation 16:3

The Third Trumpet

In the case of the third trumpet, the target area is the *fresh waters of the earth*. A great star fell from heaven on one-third of the rivers and on the springs of water. The waters became bitter, causing many people to die from drinking them. Again this star could not have been a literal star but some heavenly body burning as it passed through the earth's atmosphere. Like the previous trumpets, this affected one-third of the target area.

> ¹⁰Then the third angel sounded: And a great star fell from heaven, burning like a torch, and it fell on a third of the rivers and on the springs of water. ¹¹The name of the star is Wormwood. A third of the waters became wormwood, and many men died from the water, because it was made bitter.   —Revelation 8:10-11

The Third Bowl

In the case of the third bowl, the target area is the *fresh waters of the earth*. Like the third trumpet, this bowl was poured out on the rivers and springs of water, causing them to become blood. So the waters were not only bitter but were also turned blood red as a sign of judgment for shedding the blood of God's people.

> ⁴Then the third angel poured out his bowl on the rivers and springs of water, and they became blood. ⁵And I heard the angel of the waters saying: "You are righteous, O Lord, the One who is and who was and who is to be, because You have judged these things. ⁶For they have shed the blood of saints and prophets, and You have given them blood to drink. For it is their just due." ⁷And I heard another from the altar saying, "Even so, Lord God Almighty, true and righteous are Your judgments."
>
> —Revelation 16:4-7

The Fourth Trumpet

In the case of the fourth trumpet, the target area is the *sun, moon, and stars*. When the fourth trumpet sounded, one-third of the sun, moon, and stars were darkened so that there was no light seen from them for a third of the day and the night. Again we see that one-third of the target area was affected.

> ¹²Then the fourth angel sounded: And a third of the sun was struck, a third of the moon, and a third of the stars, so that a third of them were darkened. A third of the day did not shine, and likewise the night.   —Revelation 8:12

Notice when the fourth trumpet sounded (v. 12), nothing fell from the sky. But the dimming light of sun, moon, and stars, and consequently of both day and night, sent a signal that the worst was yet to come. This impression is confirmed by the voice of an angel announcing three even more terrible "woes" or judgments against the earth's inhabitants.

The Fourth Bowl

As in the case of the fourth trumpet, the target area is the *sun*. Just because the moon and stars are not mentioned in this bowl does not mean they were not affected. It simply means they were not included in the earthly account of this event. In this account we learn additional information concerning this event that was not mentioned in the heavenly account. The fact that the inhabitants of this earth were scorched with great heat suggests why the sole focus of the target area was the "sun." This torment caused men to blaspheme God. They also refused to repent and give glory to the God who had power over the judgments that were plaguing them.

> 8Then the fourth angel poured out his bowl on the sun, and power was given to him to scorch men with fire. 9And men were scorched with great heat, and they blasphemed the name of God who has power over these plagues; and they did not repent and give Him glory.
> —Revelation 16:8-9

We will look at the "three woes" with their counterpart bowls in the next chapter.

24

Same Story Told Twice
(part 5)

Comparing the Trumpets and Bowls (cont.)

Here we want to continue talking about the seventh seal, which is comprised of seven trumpets and bowls of judgment. In particular, we will be discussing the "three woes" which are the last three trumpets, and comparing these with the last three bowls.

The Fifth Trumpet

In the case of the fifth trumpet, the target area is the *bottomless pit*, or the abode of Satan.

> ¹Then the fifth angel sounded: And I saw a star fallen from heaven to the earth. To him was given the key to the bottomless pit. ²And he opened the bottomless pit, and smoke arose out of the pit like the smoke of a great furnace. So the sun and the air were darkened because of the smoke of the pit. —Revelation 9:1-2

Out of the smoke rising from the bottomless pit came locusts with scorpion stings in their tails. These were commanded not to harm what locusts naturally destroy, that is, green vegetation. Their targets were all humans dwelling on the earth who did not have the seal of God on their foreheads. The pain of their torment was so excruciating that men would seek death to escape the pain. However, God will not allow death to come as a means to escape this judgment, which He predetermined would last five months.

> ³Then out of the smoke locusts came upon the earth. And to them was given power, as the scorpions of the earth have power. ⁴They were commanded not to harm the grass of the earth, or any green thing, or any tree, but only those men who do not have the seal of God on their foreheads. ⁵And they were not given authority to kill them, but to torment them for five months. Their torment was like the torment of a scorpion when it strikes a man. ⁶In those days men will seek death and will not find it; they will desire to die, and death will flee from them.   —Revelation 9:3-6

Revelation 9:7-9 describes the appearance of these locusts, not from a natural perspective but from a spiritual one.

> ⁷The shape of the locusts was like horses prepared for battle. On their heads were crowns of something like gold, and their faces were like the faces of men. ⁸They had hair like women's hair, and their teeth were like lions' teeth. ⁹And they had breastplates like breastplates of iron, and the sound of their wings was like the sound of chariots with many horses running into battle.
>   —Revelation 9:7-9

From this description it is easy to see that it is not that of a natural life form but of a spiritual life form. Insects do not wear crowns on their heads, nor do they have faces like men, hair like a women, teeth like lions, or are adorned with iron breastplates. This is clearly the description of demonic spirits that are influencing and controlling these natural critters. This is further substantiated in the verse below, which speaks of their king as not only being a spirit being but also the very devil himself. The definition of the words "Abaddon" and "Apollyon" means, destroyer, angel of the bottomless pit, or Satan.

> [11]And they had as king over them the angel of the bottomless pit, whose name in Hebrew is Abaddon, but in Greek he has the name Apollyon.   —Revelation 9:11

This is the completion of the "first woe."

The Fifth Bowl

In the case of the fifth bowl, the target area is the *throne of the beast*, which is the bottomless pit, as clearly stated in the account of the fifth trumpet.

> [10]Then the fifth angel poured out his bowl on the throne of the beast, and his kingdom became full of darkness; and they gnawed their tongues because of the pain. [11]They blasphemed the God of heaven because of their pains and their sores, and did not repent of their deeds.
>   —Revelation 16:10-11

It is important to note that in each of the two perspectives, darkness covers the earth. As to the nature of the judgment inflicted on mankind in this bowl, there is very little detail.

It simply says that men gnawed their tongues because of the extreme pain. It would not be a big leap to believe that the pain and sores were the result of the scorpion-like stings of the locusts. Even with all of this torment, men would not repent of their deeds.

The Sixth Trumpet

In the case of the sixth trumpet, the target area is the *great river Euphrates.*

> [13]Then the sixth angel sounded: And I heard a voice from the four horns of the golden altar which is before God, [14]saying to the sixth angel who had the trumpet, "Release the four angels who are bound at the great river Euphrates."   —Revelation 9:13-14

The judgment as seen from a spiritual perspective claims the lives of one-third of all mankind. Their death is the result of a two-hundred-million-man army destroying everything in its path over a time period of thirteen months, one day, and one hour. Could the metaphoric language used to describe the military weapons bringing about this great slaughter be indicative of modern-day weapons of mass destruction? Could it be suggesting weapons that might include both chemical and nuclear warfare? The figurative language might lend itself for one to draw such a conclusion.

> [15]So the four angels, who had been prepared for the hour and day and month and year, were released to kill a third of mankind. [16]Now the number of the army of the horsemen was two hundred million; I heard the number of them. [17]And thus I saw the horses in the vision: those who sat on them had breastplates of fiery red, hyacinth blue, and sulfur yellow; and the heads of the horses were

like the heads of lions; and out of their mouths came fire, smoke, and brimstone. [18]By these three plagues a third of mankind was killed – by the fire and the smoke and the brimstone which came out of their mouths. [19]For their power is in their mouth and in their tails; for their tails are like serpents, having heads; and with them they do harm.   —Revelation 9:15-19

Even with all of this, men would not repent. Look at the nature of the sins men were still committing, knowing they were under the judgment of God. It is hard to believe they continued to commit such wicked sins while knowing God abhorred these. It was as though they invited yet more of God's judgments as they slapped God in the face by committing such sins as demon worship, idolatry, murders, sorceries, sexual immorality, and theft.

[20]But the rest of mankind, who were not killed by these plagues, did not repent of the works of their hands, that they should not worship demons, and idols of gold, silver, brass, stone, and wood, which can neither see nor hear nor walk. [21]And they did not repent of their murders or their sorceries or their sexual immorality or their thefts.
                          —Revelation 9:20-21

This is the completion of the "second woe," and the "third woe" will be quickly following on its heels.

[14]The second woe is past. Behold, the third woe is coming quickly.   —Revelation 11:14

The Sixth Bowl

In the case of the sixth bowl, the target area once again is the *great river Euphrates*. The Euphrates River will dry up, making an easy path for the kings of the East to move their massive armies to be staged in the Megiddo Valley near Jerusalem. They will join with all the other armies of the world bent on destroying Israel and the Holy City.

> [12]Then the sixth angel poured out his bowl on the great river Euphrates, and its water was dried up, so that the way of the kings from the east might be prepared. [13]And I saw three unclean spirits like frogs coming out of the mouth of the dragon, out of the mouth of the beast, and out of the mouth of the false prophet. [14]For they are spirits of demons, performing signs, which go out to the kings of the earth and of the whole world, to gather them to the battle of that great day of God Almighty.

> [15]"Behold, I am coming as a thief. Blessed is he who watches, and keeps his garments, lest he walk naked and they see his shame."

> [16]And they gathered them together to the place called in Hebrew, Armageddon.   —Revelation 16:12-16

Even from a natural or earthly perspective, we can see the supernatural involvement of the spiritual world influencing all the nations to gather their armies against Israel. This spiritual influence comes from three unclean spirits coming out of the mouths of Satan, the beast, and the false prophet. These are described as demons performing great signs before all the kings of the earth and of the whole world to draw them into the great battle of Armageddon (the war of the Megiddo Valley). God puts a hook in the jaws of all the nations by allowing these spirits to draw them to Jerusalem like vultures are drawn to a carcass. This sets the stage for the "third woe," where God and His armies will fight with the remnant of Israel against all the nations of the world.

The Seventh Trumpet

In the case of the seventh trumpet, the target area is, at first sight, a little ambiguous. However, if we read carefully and compare it with the seventh bowl, we can see what is implied.

> [15]Then the seventh angel sounded: And there were loud voices in heaven, saying, "The kingdoms of this world have become the kingdoms of our Lord and of His Christ, and He shall reign forever and ever!" [16]And the twenty-four elders who sat before God on their thrones fell on their faces and worshiped God, [17]saying:
>
> "We give You thanks, O Lord God Almighty, the One who is and who was and who is to come, because You have taken Your great power and reigned. [18]The nations were angry, and Your wrath has come, and the time of the dead, that they should be judged, and that You should reward Your servants the prophets and the saints, and those who fear Your name, small and great, and should destroy those who destroy the earth."   —Revelation 11:15-18

To determine the target area of this trumpet, we need to focus on what is happening to know where it is taking place. The first verses of this passage simply deal with the reaction of those in heaven at the sounding of the seventh trumpet. However, in verse 18 above, we finally see an event taking place which reveals the target area. It says that it was a time when the dead would come out of their graves to be judged. It was a time when the prophets and the saints should receive their rewards. When does this happen? It happens when we meet Jesus at the rapture of the church. Where does it happen? It happens in the air as declared in 1 Thessalonians 4:13-18:

[13]But I do not want you to be ignorant, brethren, concerning those who have fallen asleep, lest you sorrow as others who have no hope. [14]For if we believe that Jesus died and rose again, even so God will bring with Him those who sleep in Jesus. [15]For this we say to you by the word of the Lord, that we who are alive and remain until the coming of the Lord will by no means precede those who are asleep. [16]For the Lord Himself will descend from heaven with a shout, with the voice of an archangel, and with the trumpet of God. And the dead in Christ will rise first. [17]Then we who are alive and remain shall be caught up together with them in the clouds to meet the Lord in the air. And thus we shall always be with the Lord. [18]Therefore comfort one another with these words.

—1 Thessalonians 4:13-18

Notice that it says that the Lord will descend from heaven with a shout, with the voice of an archangel and with the trumpet of God. At the seventh or last trumpet the saints, dead and alive, will meet the Lord in the air and forever be with Him.

In the case of the seventh trumpet, the target area is the *air*. The seventh bowl confirms this conclusion.

The Seventh Bowl

In the case of the seventh bowl, the target area is the *air*.

[17]Then the seventh angel poured out his bowl into the air, and a loud voice came out of the temple of heaven, from the throne, saying, "It is done!"

—Revelation 16:17

Notice that the voice from heaven said, "It is done!" The same thing is said in the heavenly account of this event in Revelation 10.

⁷But in the days of the voice of the seventh angel, when he shall begin to sound, the mystery of God should be finished, as he has declared to his servants the prophets.
—Revelation 10:7 KJV

The Greek word for "sound" in this verse is *salpizzo* which means "to sound a trumpet." I believe the mystery being spoken of here is none other than the mystery described in 1 Corinthians 15.

⁵¹Behold, I tell you a mystery: We shall not all sleep, but we shall all be changed – ⁵²in a moment, in the twinkling of an eye, at the last trumpet. For the trumpet will sound, and the dead will be raised incorruptible, and we shall be changed.   —1 Corinthians 15:51-52

Other Similarities Between the Seventh Trumpet and Seventh Bowl

As we discussed earlier in this book, there were five common perceivable activities that occurred in both the seventh trumpet and the seventh bowl. They were lightnings, voices, thunderings, strong earthquake, and great hail. These can be seen clearly in the two passages below. These further substantiate that the seventh trumpet and seventh bowl are speaking of the same event from two different perspectives.

Seventh Trumpet

¹⁹And the temple of God was opened in heaven, and there was seen in his temple the ark of his testament: and there were *lightnings*, and *voices*, and *thunderings*, and an *earthquake*, and *great hail*.   —Revelation 11:19 KJV

Seventh Bowl

> [18]And there were *voices*, and *thunders*, and *lightnings*; and there was a *great earthquake*, such as was not since men were upon the earth, so mighty an earthquake, and so great. [19]And the great city was divided into three parts, and the cities of the nations fell: and great Babylon came in remembrance before God, to give unto her the cup of the wine of the fierceness of his wrath. [20]And every island fled away, and the mountains were not found. [21]And there fell upon men a *great hail* out of heaven, every stone about the weight of a talent: and men blasphemed God because of the plague of the hail; for the plague thereof was exceeding great.　　—Revelation 16:18-21 KJV

The seventh trumpet and bowl concludes with the same story being told twice from two different perspectives. What follows after this is the judgment seat of Christ, the marriage supper of the Lamb, the second coming of Christ, the setting up of the millennial kingdom, the great white throne judgment, and the eternal state when time will be no more. These are only mentioned after the second telling of the story from the earthly perspective. We will discuss these in the following chapters, along with several other topics not previously covered, such as the two witnesses, Mystery Babylon, and the marriage of Christ to His bride.

25

The Two Witnesses

Introduction

The story told twice covers the period of time from the revelation and opening of the seven seals through the sounding and the impact of the last trumpet and bowl. There are several things that occur in that time frame which we have not previously discussed. One of the reasons for this is that these are included in only one perspective. The first example, the two witnesses, is only seen in the first telling of the story. Other examples include Mystery Babylon, the catching away of the church, the judgment seat of Christ, the marriage of Christ to His bride, the millennial kingdom, the great white throne judgment, and the eternal state. We will briefly discuss each of these before concluding this section of the book.

The Two Witnesses

The only New Testament account of the two witnesses is found in Revelation chapter 11. When it comes to the identity of the two witnesses described in this chapter, there are several popular theological views. The more popular views would include the following. Some see the two witnesses as being representative of the Jewish and Gentile church. Some view them as a visible representation of the church that is alive in the last days. One of the most popular views is that these are none other than Moses and Elijah. I want to make a disclaimer at the outset of sharing my position as to who the two witnesses are. My position was not arrived at by a revelation I received from God. It is based on my best understanding (opinion) of which view most satisfies the Scriptures.

It is not my goal in this writing to cover each of these positions in great detail. I neither want to give the space or time needed to do so. I will briefly share the reason why I reject each view before sharing the view which I can most identify with. Let us first look at the entire passage of Revelation 11:3-14 below before making remarks on the content of specific verses.

> ³"And I will give power to my two witnesses, and they will prophesy one thousand two hundred and sixty days, clothed in sackcloth." ⁴These are the two olive trees and the two lampstands standing before the God of the earth. ⁵And if anyone wants to harm them, fire proceeds from their mouth and devours their enemies. And if anyone wants to harm them, he must be killed in this manner. ⁶These have power to shut heaven, so that no rain falls in the days of their prophecy; and they have power over waters to turn them to blood, and to strike the earth with all plagues, as often as they desire. ⁷When they finish their testimony, the beast that ascends out of the bottomless pit will make war against them, overcome them, and kill them. ⁸And their dead bodies will lie in the street of the great city, which spiritually is called Sodom and Egypt, where also our Lord was crucified. ⁹Then those from the

peoples, tribes, tongues, and nations will see their dead bodies three-and-a-half days, and not allow their dead bodies to be put into graves. [10]And those who dwell on the earth will rejoice over them, make merry, and send gifts to one another, because these two prophets tormented those who dwell on the earth. [11]Now after the three-and-a-half days the breath of life from God entered them, and they stood on their feet, and great fear fell on those who saw them. [12]And they heard a loud voice from heaven saying to them, "Come up here." And they ascended to heaven in a cloud, and their enemies saw them. [13]In the same hour there was a great earthquake, and a tenth of the city fell. In the earthquake seven thousand people were killed, and the rest were afraid and gave glory to the God of heaven. [14]The second woe is past. Behold, the third woe is coming quickly.

—Revelation 11:3-14

What do we know about these two witnesses from the information given in this passage of Scripture? We know that they are the personal witnesses of the angel speaking in Revelation chapters 10 and 11. I believe this angel, clothed with a rainbow on his head, whose face did shine like the sun and whose feet were as pillars of fire, is none other than Jesus. We know that John said they were alive in his day standing before the God of the earth. We know that they are prophets (Revelation 11:3,10) and that they will prophesy 1,260 days. We know that the two witnesses are called olive trees and lampstands, which is an indicator of their role. Their role is to be a light fueled by the olive oil, which is symbolic of the anointing of the Holy Spirit. As lights, they are to be a witness against their enemies concerning the coming judgments of God. They declare these judgments and then prophesy them into existence. We know that prior to the unveiling of the two witnesses, Satan will raise up his own two witnesses, the beast and false prophet. God's answer to Satan's plan is that He likewise will present His two witnesses to the world. We know that they are invincible while they are prophesying their judgments. However, when they have finished their witness after the 1,260 days, they become vulnerable to the beast, who kills them and leaves them to lie unburied in the streets for 3½ days. It would seem from Revelation 11:8 that their death occurs in Jerusalem and most likely by crucifixion, as was also true of the Lord. They are then raised from the dead and caught up to heaven to be with God. This happens in plain view of the very enemies they tormented. Their resurrection is not from the grave, like Jesus' resurrection, because their bodies were never buried. We also know the time frame of their ministry and death from Revelation 11:14, which declares that this is all a part of the "second woe." Revelation chapters 8 and 9 clearly define this woe as the sixth trumpet of judgment. It goes on to say that the "third woe," which is the seventh and last trumpet, follows quickly.

Now let us look at some of the more widely held views:

The Jewish and Gentile Church

These proponents conclude that since much of the language used in the book of Revelation is symbolic, it is reasonable to suggest that the two olive trees are symbolic of the Jewish and Gentile churches. They cite the two olive trees spoken of in Romans 11. The natural olive tree would be symbolic of the Jews and the wild olive tree of the Gentiles. Though this is a logical conclusion, it is illogical to think that during the sixth trumpet all the members of all the churches throughout the world would be killed and left unburied for 3½ days. For this reason, the concept of the two witnesses being corporate bodies is highly unlikely. In addition to this, there is no Jewish or Gentile church as separate entities, according to God's very definition of the church. He says that the church is neither Jew nor Gentile, bond nor free, male nor female. It is composed of all those who receive Jesus as the Messiah and are born of Him. Remember, Zechariah clearly teaches that the Jews as a people group will not see and embrace Jesus as their Messiah until He comes again with His saints during the battle of Armageddon.

The Last Days Church

These proponents point out that the message of the book of Revelation is directed to the church, as stated in Revelation chapter 1. They cite the many metaphors used to refer to the church as proof that the church is the central focus of this book. Some examples of such are the seven lampstands, the city of God, and the bride of Christ. However, for the same reason as stated in the previous view, it is highly unlikely that any corporate entity could meet the criteria set forth in this passage of Scripture. The fact that they are actual preachers and not corporate symbols of institutions or movements is indicated by the description of their clothing and behavior. It's hard to imagine the entirety of the corporate church walking about in sackcloth and prophesying for 1,260 contiguous days.

Moses and Elijah

Those who hold to this view have a very strong case. They conclude that the miracles, signs, wonders, and judgments these two prophets did are identical with those that the two witnesses are described as doing. They have power to shut up the heavens so that it will not rain for 3½ years, and power to call down fire to consume their enemies even as did Elijah. They have power over the waters to turn them to blood and to call down plagues upon the earth even as did Moses. Even with all of these factors, I feel there is a stronger case to be made for yet another viewpoint. The case that I am referring to is that of Enoch and Elijah.

Enoch and Elijah

The strongest case for the two witnesses being Enoch and Elijah is that these were the only two men in the history of mankind to not taste death. Enoch and Elijah were both translated. Could it be that their deaths were to be deferred until the end of this age as the two witnesses?

Hebrews 9:27 clearly states, "It is appointed unto men once to die, but after this the judgment." The only exceptions to this rule are those who are alive and remain at the catching away of the church near the end of this age. Enoch is found in faith's "hall of fame" in Hebrews 11. This passage declares that Enoch did not see death and was not found, because God had taken him away. Genesis 5 says that Enoch walked with God. He was a diligent God-seeker, not a man-pleaser. History records him as a man who lived a separated life and only related to mankind as a prophet sent to reprove and warn the wicked.

> ⁵By faith Enoch was taken away so that he did not see death, "and was not found, because God had taken him"; for before he was taken he had this testimony, that he pleased God. ⁶But without faith it is impossible to please Him, for he who comes to God must believe that He is,

and that He is a rewarder of those who diligently seek Him.   —Hebrews 11:5-6

To the contrary, Moses died, which is born witness to when the archangel Michael disputed with Satan over his body. The location of the body of Moses was found on the earth by spiritual beings and was fought over to secure its possession. For Moses to return as one of the two witnesses, it would mean he would have to die twice, not once. However, there is nothing in the Scriptures to suggest that Enoch and Elijah have put on incorruption and immortality. For them to die at the end of this age at the hands of the beast would not violate the Scriptures. How does all of this work? We must understand that God's ways and thoughts are not ours. His are much higher than ours. Therefore, it would be futile for us to try to understand what Paul describes as the depths and riches of the wisdom of God. He says that God's ways are unsearchable and past finding out. The Word of God simply declares that these two left the earth without dying. Could it be that their deaths were only deferred to another time? Accepting Elijah as one of the two witnesses is an easy chore, but what about Enoch? Was he, too, a prophet? Was his ministry also to be a light in the midst of a dark time while warning of impending judgment? Did he even know much about eschatology? The New Testament answers these questions in the book of Jude.

[14]Now Enoch, the seventh from Adam, prophesied about these men also, saying, "Behold, the Lord comes with ten thousands of His saints, [15]to execute judgment on all, to convict all who are ungodly among them of all their ungodly deeds which they have committed in an ungodly way, and of all the harsh things which ungodly sinners have spoken against Him.   —Jude 1:14-15

From this passage we can see that Enoch was indeed a prophet who prophesied about what would happen in the end times. He was the great prophet before the flood. Elijah was the great prophet after the flood. The old world had no Jews. Enoch was a witness to the Gentile world and the Gentile church, even as Elijah was to the Jewish nation and the redeemed of Israel. I believe both of these will reappear near the end of this age to once again be anointed lights and witnesses to both Gentile and Jew.

Prophecy does not necessarily only refer to predicting the future. The primary meaning of *prophecy* is "to speak forth," "to proclaim," or "to preach." The two witnesses will proclaim to the world that the disasters occurring during the last 3½ years of this age are the judgments of God for their wickedness. I believe that according to their words and by their words will the plagues and judgments come. They will warn that God's final outpouring of judgment and eternal hell will follow. In my estimation, no two greater lights and witnesses spanning the time of the worlds before and after the flood capture the essence of God's two witnesses as do Enoch and Elijah.

In conclusion, I believe Enoch is a better choice than Moses, because Enoch's return to this earth does not violate any principle of Scripture whereas Moses would have to die twice if he were to be the choice.

26

Mystery Babylon – The Great Harlot

Introduction

One of the main characters in the dramatic events of the last days is Mystery Babylon. Her role is not only significant in the last days, but she has also been a major influence for hundreds of years leading up to this present hour. When the fall of Mystery Babylon is announced, the world will be shocked and horrified by her destruction. So significant is the falling of Mystery Babylon that the book of Revelation devotes two whole chapters to this event and mentions it briefly in two other chapters. In addition to Revelation, it is prophesied in great length in both Isaiah and Jeremiah. Much of the language in Revelation chapters 17 and 18 is taken almost verbatim out of the prophecies of Isaiah and Jeremiah.

Mystery Babylon

The first mention of her is found in Revelation chapter 14:

> [8]And another angel followed, saying, "Babylon is fallen, is fallen, that great city, because she has made all nations drink of the wine of the wrath of her fornication."
> —Revelation 14:8

This verse describes her as a great city that falls because she caused all nations to be influenced and polluted by her fornication. I believe the fornication being spoken of here is primarily about spiritual uncleanness and unfaithfulness to the one true God. Certainly that would also affect the sexual morality of many within any society.

One of the first things to take note of is that she is described as a mystery. The woman, Mystery Babylon, is truly a mystery without spiritual discernment. It is a mystery except for the ones who are spiritually clued in through spiritual revelation. The same is true of the city of God; she is a mystery except to those who are spiritually clued in through revelation. Two of the most popular schools of thought as to the identity of this woman are *America* or the *Catholic church*. For reasons we shall later explain as we delve into the many clues listed, I want to say that I do not believe either of these views is correct. She is not America nor is she the Catholic church. Both of these may indeed have relevance as typological fulfillments, but I do not believe that either of them is the ultimate prophetic fulfillment that God is speaking of in the prophecies concerning Mystery Babylon.

Let us now look at some of the clues given as to her identity.

Who She Is and Is Not

It is beneficial now to read a portion of Scripture that harbors several important clues as to the identity of Mystery Babylon.

³So he carried me away in the Spirit into the wilderness. And I saw a woman sitting on a scarlet beast, which was full of names of blasphemy, having seven heads and ten horns. ⁴The woman was arrayed in purple and scarlet, and adorned with gold and precious stones and pearls, having in her hand a golden cup full of abominations and the filthiness of her fornication. ⁵And on her forehead a name was written: MYSTERY, BABYLON THE GREAT, THE MOTHER OF HARLOTS AND OF THE ABOMINATIONS OF THE EARTH.

⁶I saw the woman, drunk with the blood of the saints and with the blood of the martyrs of Jesus. And when I saw her, I marveled with great amazement. ⁷But the angel said to me, "Why did you marvel? I will tell you the mystery of the woman and of the beast that carries her, which has the seven heads and the ten horns. ⁸The beast that you saw was, and is not, and will ascend out of the bottomless pit and go to perdition. And those who dwell on the earth will marvel, whose names are not written in the Book of Life from the foundation of the world, when they see the beast that was, and is not, and yet is. ⁹Here is the mind which has wisdom: The seven heads are seven mountains on which the woman sits. ¹⁰There are also seven kings. Five have fallen, one is, and the other has not yet come. And when he comes, he must continue a short time. ¹¹The beast that was, and is not, is himself also the eighth, and is of the seven, and is going to perdition. ¹²The ten horns which you saw are ten kings who have received no kingdom as yet, but they receive authority for one hour as kings with the beast." —Revelation 17:3-12

It is said of this woman that she is clothed in purple and scarlet. She sits and is carried on the back of a scarlet-colored beast that has seven heads and ten horns. This is the same beast identified in Revelation chapter 12 as the great red dragon, and as the beast that rises up out the sea in Revelation chapter 13. The seven heads represent the seven empires that coexist with Israel and the church from their inception to the end of this age. The first empire that existed after Israel was birthed as a people was Egypt, then Assyria, then Babylon, then the Medes and Persians, then Greece, then Rome, and finally the beast. This woman rides the seven-headed beast, which spans a time from Egypt to the beast of the last days. Whoever this woman is, she also has to be in existence to span that same period of time if she is to be carried on the back of all that this beast was and is. This fact alone would disqualify America and the Catholic church as being the ultimate fulfillment of this prophecy. Both of these were not even in existence until after six of the seven empires had come and gone.

It is also said of her that she is a great harlot. She is declared to be the mother of harlots and the mother of the abominations of the earth. History is clear that there were spiritual harlotries and earthly abominations that were a stench to God during the first six empires prior to existence of America and the Catholic church. She is not the Roman Catholic church. Romanism and all other external religious systems before and after Rome came from this mother and grew up alongside the true church as a religious parasite. This spiritual parasite emerges in the church like a Jezebel in Thyatira. She does this to infiltrate the church with counterfeit, church-like tares in the midst of wheat. Mystery Babylon bears a relationship to the beast as does the true church to Christ. She is a mock religious system of true Judaeo/Christian worship. This woman is said to be drunk with the blood of the martyrs since the martyrdom of Cain. This blood dates back long before the formation of the Catholic church. Jesus cited one such example when He introduced Jerusalem as the city that killed His prophets. Again this happened long before the emergence of America or the Catholic church.

> [34]"Oh Jerusalem, Jerusalem, the one who kills the prophets and stones those who are sent to her! How often I wanted to gather your children together, as a hen gathers her brood under her wings, but you were not willing!
> —Luke 13:34

The Catholic church is just one example of many churches being infected with Satan's counterfeit religious system. Don't think she has a monopoly on external, ritualistic worship. She has many predecessors and contemporaries. There are professing evangelicals, fundamentalists, Pentecostals and, yes, even charismatics that are infected with this type of worship. There is no right or wrong denomination or church. There are just people who attend these churches, some of which know God and have a genuine relationship with Him and some who don't. It's not about the denomination or church. It's entirely about the people who attend them. Matthew 7 epitomizes the religious system of the harlot.

> [21]"Not everyone who says to Me, 'Lord, Lord,' shall enter the kingdom of heaven, but he who does the will of My Father in heaven. [22]Many will say to Me in that day, 'Lord, Lord, have we not prophesied in Your name, cast out demons in Your name, and done many wonders in Your name?' [23]And then I will declare to them, 'I never knew you; depart from Me, you who practice lawlessness!'"
> —Matthew 7:21-23

Notice that even though these professing believers prophesied, cast out demons, and did miracles in the name of Jesus, He denied knowing them and commanded them to depart because they were workers of iniquity. They built their houses on sand. Their relationship was shallow. They failed to dig deeper through all the religious shifting sand to be grounded on the rock of Christ. These will not be a part of the woman clothed with sun, but rather a part of the counterfeit religious system of Babylon. The problem is that because of deception, they do not realize their condition until it is too late to correct. However, those who are firmly grounded on the rock will not fail in the time of testing and tribulation. Matthew 24:9-13 shows both women growing together as a part of the Christian church. However, when they are cast into great tribulation and hated by the world for His name's sake, a separating will come that reveals the true and exposes the false. Many who attended church together will be offended or scandalized and will betray the true woman with whom they once used to worship. God will use the great tribulation period to finally draw a clear line of demarcation between these two women.

The religious woman will not suffer for Jesus' namesake but rather will seek to avoid it by snuggling up to, being loyal to, and even being a worshipper of the miracle-working antichrist and false prophet. Because of her strong desire to be preeminent, her insatiable appetite for the lusts of the flesh, and her indomitable pursuit of a life of ease, comfort, and pleasure, the beast will be more than happy to carry her on his back. This woman is more commerce-driven than spirit-driven. This makes her more profitable and compatible with the world than does the true church. Wealth and leisure spawn immorality and every evil work bent on satisfying and sustaining its self-indulgent lifestyle. These are the very traits that keep her distracted from pursuing a true, intimate relationship with God while at the same time soothing her conscience with the pursuit of religion.

This woman is more than willing to move the ancient landmarks of the patriarchs and compromise the standards and pillars on which the true church is to stand. However, the woman of promise knows her role is to be the pillar and ground of truth. She accepts, as her mission, both to model and promote conduct and behavior congruent to such. Representatives of God who swear allegiance to Him ought to know that He and His standards change not; He is the same yesterday, today, and forever.

Whenever and wherever true Judeo/Christian worship has existed, Satan has always been busy infiltrating to contaminate their purity of devotion to God. He does this by leading "nominal" Christians to labor in the same fields into which God leads His children to labor. Often they are oblivious to what they are doing and for whom they are working. This they do as they faithfully attend and support the very churches to which you and I might also be called to serve. This is the anti-church disguised as being part of the true church. Often they are the instigators of the persecution and ridicule of the devout. They paint true devotion as extremism and being beyond the pale (outside the boundaries of acceptable behavior). As is true of the tares growing alongside the wheat, so these compete for and even steal the time, ministry, and life God intended to be bread for the children of God. They consume the children's bread to impede growth and vitality all the while masquerading as one of their fellow servants. Nevertheless, her true nature as a servant is to serve herself at the expense of any and all. This nature has always caused this harlot of the ages to seduce the precious life within the church. Her target is the little lambs. Most often she operates in the same spirit that manifested in Absalom or in Jezebel. She is the antithesis of the woman clothed with the sun, spoken of in Revelation chapter 12. There has been enmity between these two women since religion began infiltrating man's relationship with God both before and after the flood. Because of this, there has been and always will be an internal struggle between these two women within God's assembly of called-out ones. The one answers to the Jerusalem of this age, which ensnares her and her children into bondage. The other woman, who answers to the Jerusalem which is from above, is free and is the mother of all true believers in the one true God.

> **For this Hagar [woman] is mount Sinai in Arabia, and answers to Jerusalem, which now is, and is in bondage with her children. But Jerusalem which is above [the other woman] is free, which is the mother of us all.**
> **—Galatians 4:25-26 KJV**

The Judeo-Christian saga has been filled with the ongoing struggle of these two women. It is a tale of two women that is noteworthy enough to be given careful consideration as they approach their final showdown at the end of the age.

The Tale of Two Women

Let us now take a moment to contrast these two women. Both are mothers. The first brought forth an overcoming son to rule while the second birthed harlots and abominations. The first had rule over the powers of darkness while the second had rule over earthly kingdoms and kings. The first is pure while the second is a harlot. The first is a covenant keeper while the second is a covenant breaker. The first is carried on wings of the Holy Spirit while the second is carried on the back of the great red dragon. The first becomes a heavenly city adorned as a wife for Christ while the second becomes an earthly city joined to the beast and fit for destruction. The first is the church of the Christ while the second is the church of the antichrist.

The many abominations of the harlot begs the question, "Why doesn't God judge her speedily?" The answer is that God does not judge anything before its time. Both women have to come into the fullness of what God has purposed for them. He wants the tares and the wheat to grow together until they come unto maturity, at which time God will harvest them both for their predestined purposes and ends at the close of the age. His predetermined reaping order in the last days is – the tares first, followed by the wheat.

The Fall of Babylon

As we continue looking at the story of the harlot in Revelation 17, we will see her end demise as she receives her just reward.

12"The ten horns which you saw are ten kings who have received no kingdom as yet, but they receive authority for one hour as kings with the beast. 13These are of one mind, and they will give their power and authority to the beast. 14These will make war with the Lamb, and the Lamb will overcome them, for He is Lord of lords and King of kings; and those who are with Him are called, chosen, and faithful." 15Then he said to me, "The waters which you saw, where the harlot sits, are peoples, multitudes, nations, and tongues. 16And the ten horns which you saw on the beast, these will hate the harlot, make her desolate and naked, eat her flesh and burn her with fire. 17For God has put it into their hearts to fulfill His purpose, to be of one mind, and to give their kingdom to the beast, until the words of God are fulfilled. [18]And the woman whom you saw is that great city which reigns over the kings of the earth."   —Revelation 17:12-18

As we look at this passage in chronological order, we see the ten kings receiving authority for a short season with the beast. These are of one mind to give their power and authority to the beast. Even though the harlot has related to and been carried on the back of the beast approximately 3,000 years, these ten kings will hate her. Why? This woman is described as that great city that reigns over the kings of the earth. Though she reigns over these newly ordained kings, it is obvious that such reign is odious and unwelcomed by them. What causes this sudden change of attitude toward Mystery Babylon? I believe the answer can be found in Revelation chapter 13. There it states that the false prophet, who worked great miracles, will make an image of the beast that comes alive and speaks. He will then demand everyone to worship this idol of the beast. This does away with all other forms of worship in the world. Those who will not worship according to this newly set up religion will be executed. The ten kings, who swear allegiance to the beast, will hate the harlot. They will hate her long exercised, controlling, religious system, which conflicts with the newly established form of worship. Her usefulness no longer serves the empire's purposes. I believe it is because of this that they shall strip her completely, burn her with fire, and make her desolate. This proves the point we made earlier that God restrains judgment until the cup of abomination is full. This He does in order to fulfill His purpose.

[17]For God has put it into their hearts to fulfill His purpose, to be of one mind, and to give their kingdom to the

beast, until the words of God are fulfilled.

—Revelation 17:17

After they finish destroying Babylon, they join with the beast to make war with the Lamb, and the Lamb shall overcome them. This concludes the story of the great harlot and the empire of the beast in this age. Though Revelation chapter 18 talks more about this subject, it merely adds greater detail to the story that was previously told. Whereas Revelation chapter 17 describes the harlot over the course of her entire existence, Revelation 18 primarily focuses on her last days during the seventh empire of the beast.

More Details

After the telling of the story in Revelation 17, an angel comes down from heaven and announces the doom that has just happened.

> [1]After these things I saw another angel coming down from heaven, having great authority, and the earth was illuminated with his glory. [2]And he cried mightily with a loud voice, saying, "Babylon the great is fallen, is fallen, and has become a dwelling place of demons, a prison for every foul spirit, and a cage for every unclean and hated bird! [3]For all the nations have drunk of the wine of the wrath of her fornication, the kings of the earth have committed fornication with her, and the merchants of the earth have become rich through the abundance of her luxury."   —Revelation 18:1-3

This announcement by the angel in Revelation 18:2 is like that of Revelation 14:8 in which it is declared, "Babylon is fallen, is fallen." Notice that the word "fallen" is repeated and appears twice in each declaration. The same is true in Isaiah 21:9.

> [9]"And look, here comes a chariot of men with a pair of horsemen!" Then he answered and said, "Babylon is fallen, is fallen! And all the carved images of her gods he has broken to the ground."   —Isaiah 21:9

In all three passages, it is said that "Babylon is fallen, is fallen." I believe this emphasis is not accidental or coincidental. It is the same hermeneutic used by John in describing the seven trumpets of the seventh seal. After he introduces the first four trumpets, he utters, "woe, woe, woe" (Revelation 8:13) concerning the remaining three. This was for emphasis. It was to mark them as three separate dreadful events. Likewise, in the case of "Babylon is fallen, is fallen," I believe it speaks of two distinct fallings: 1) the religious system, and 2) the religious center or city.

This leads us to the question of whether or not there will be a city established as the new headquarters of this false religious system. I personally believe that there might be a union of nominal Christianity with Islam in the near future and that their headquarters might be reestablished in Babylon where it all started. The reason I believe this is that the prophecies concerning Babylon have yet to be fulfilled. Babylon's final destruction is prophesied to be irreversible. No one will ever live there again. Currently there is a literal city occupying part of the very ground where Babylon was before its destruction. After her final destruction, it is prophesied that never again will she be inhabited.

> [39]"Therefore the wild desert beasts shall dwell there with the jackals, and the ostriches shall dwell in it. It shall be inhabited no more forever, nor shall it be dwelt in from generation to generation. [40]As God overthrew Sodom and Gomorrah and their neighbors," says the Lord, "So

no one shall reside there, nor son of man dwell in it."
—Jeremiah 50:39-40

Couple this with the fact that this city has had a history of religious abominations and defiance of God as well as merciless atrocities against the people of God. It is in Babylon, formerly known as Babel, that Nimrod unified the people to build a tower to intrude into heaven. It was also the capital of the Babylonian empire which literally laid waste to Jerusalem and plundered the holy things of God. I believe in these last days when she becomes the center of the false religious system that opposes all that God stands for, He will reward her double for all that she has done. God doesn't forget these abominable things and has prophesied concerning Babylon's total and permanent destruction in the future.

> [4]And I heard another voice from heaven saying, "Come out of her, my people, lest you share in her sins, and lest you receive of her plagues. [5]For her sins have reached to heaven, and God has remembered her iniquities. [6]Render to her just as she rendered to you, and repay her double according to her works; in the cup which she has mixed, mix double for her. [7]In the measure that she glorified herself and lived luxuriously, in the same measure give her torment and sorrow; for she says in her heart, 'I sit as queen, and am no widow, and will not see sorrow.' [8]Therefore her plagues will come in one day – death and mourning and famine. And she will be utterly burned with fire, for strong is the Lord God who judges her."   —Revelation 18:4-8

Notice the strong exhortation God cries out to His people to come out of Mystery Babylon. Do you really believe He is asking all of His children to leave America or the Catholic church? That would be nigh unto impossible. I do believe it is very probable that He could be instructing any of His children who are residing in the actual city of Babylon to come out of her before her total destruction. God did no less with Lot and his family before He totally destroyed forever the cities of Sodom and Gomorrah.

> [21]Then a mighty angel took up a stone like a great millstone and threw it into the sea, saying, "Thus with violence the great city Babylon shall be thrown down, and shall not be found anymore.   —Revelation 18:21

Whoever you think Mystery Babylon might be, this one thing is sure. She will be a well-known entity in the last days. So tangible and evident will she be that the whole world will be aware of her demise. They will be cast into a state of shock and greatly mourn her destruction.

27

The Rapture and After
(part 1)

Introduction

In the remaining chapters, we discuss various events that take place after the sounding of the last trumpet up to and including the eternal state when time will be no more.

The Rapture

One of the age old questions is, "When does the rapture of the church happen?" As we have already shown from the Scriptures, it happens after the seventh trumpet sounds. It is not our intention to review the scriptural case we made previously, but rather to give a general description of this event and of its earthly impact.

At the time of the rapture, the Lord will descend out of heaven with a shout, with the voice of the archangel, and with the trumpet of God. At the sounding of this trumpet, the dead in Christ will rise first, and then those who are alive and remaining on the earth will be caught up together with them in the clouds to meet Him in the *air*. Remember, the target area of the seventh bowl, the same event as the seventh trumpet, is the *air*. What impact will this event have on the inhabitants living on the earth? I believe it will be a multiplied version of the reaction that occurred when the two witnesses were caught up to God. Those left behind were greatly terrified and gave glory to the God of heaven. This event leaves not one saint remaining upon the earth or under the earth. Imagine a world that does not have even one person who has been born of God residing there. The following Scriptures describe this great event:

> [51]Behold, I tell you a mystery: We shall not all sleep, but we shall all be changed– [52]in a moment, in the twinkling of an eye, at the last trumpet. For the trumpet will sound, and the dead will be raised incorruptible, and we shall be changed. [53]For this corruptible must put on incorruption, and this mortal must put on immortality. [54]So when this corruptible has put on incorruption, and this mortal has put on immortality, then shall be brought to pass the saying that is written: "Death is swallowed up in victory." [55]"O Death, where is your sting? O Hades, where is your victory?"   —1 Corinthians 15:51-55

> [15]For this we say to you by the word of the Lord, that we who are alive and remain until the coming of the Lord will by no means precede those who are asleep. [16]For the Lord Himself will descend from heaven with a shout, with the voice of an archangel, and with the trumpet of God. And the dead in Christ will rise first. [17]Then we who are alive and remain shall be caught up together with them in the clouds to meet the Lord in the air. And thus we shall always be with the Lord.
>   —1 Thessalonians 4:15-17

It is important to remember that the rapture of the church is not the same as the second coming of Christ. These are two distinctly different events with respect to both timing and purpose.

The Judgment Seat of Christ

The judgment seat of Christ, often referred to as the Behma, is the judgment of the works of those who belong to Christ from the beginning of time unto the rapture. The word *behma* in the Greek simply means "judgment seat." This judgment is not about personal "identity" but rather, personal "achievement." It's not about whether you are a believer or nonbeliever, but rather it is about the quality of your works as a believer. It is the judgment of the righteous who lived prior to and up to the rapture or catching away of the church.

As Paul was addressing Christians in Romans 14:10-12, he said that we will all stand before God's judgment seat and will give an account of ourselves to God. Also in speaking to believers in 2 Corinthians 5:10, he said that we must all appear before the judgment seat of Christ so that each of us may receive what is due us for the things done while in the body, whether good or bad.

> [9]Therefore we make it our aim, whether present or absent, to be well pleasing to Him. [10]For we must all appear before the judgment seat of Christ, that each one may receive the things done in the body, according to what he has done, whether good or bad. [11]Knowing, therefore, the terror of the Lord, we persuade men; but we are well known to God, and I also trust are well known in your consciences. —2 Corinthians 5:9-11

The judgment seat of Christ does not determine salvation. Its purpose is to reward His children for their faithful works while here on earth. We should not look at the judgment seat of Christ as God judging our sins, but rather as God judging our works. This judgment of our lives of service to Him and His kingdom will result in receiving rewards or suffering the loss thereof. The rewards we will receive will come in the form of degrees of rule and authority in the millennial kingdom, as well as various types of "crowns" specific to various achievements while serving God on this earth. We will one day cast our crowns at the feet of Jesus to honor Him and to make a declaration that all our good works were the result of Him and His working in and through us.

> [12]Now if anyone builds on this foundation with gold, silver, precious stones, wood, hay, straw, [13]each one's work will become clear; for the Day will declare it, because it will be revealed by fire; and the fire will test each one's work, of what sort it is. [14]If anyone's work which he has built on it endures, he will receive a reward. [15]If anyone's work is burned, he will suffer loss; but he himself will be saved, yet so as through fire.   —1 Corinthians 3:12-15

These rewards are based not only on our faithfulness, but also on our intentions and the motives of our hearts when doing our works. The judgment seat of Christ, therefore, involves believers giving an account of their lives to Christ.

When will the judgment seat of Christ occur? This judgment will occur immediately following the rapture, when all saints, dead and alive, will be caught up in the air to forever be with Jesus. The timing of the judgment seat of Christ is given in the following Scriptures:

8Finally, there is laid up for me the crown of righteousness, which the Lord, the righteous Judge, will give to me on that Day, and not to me only but also to all who have loved His appearing.   —2 Timothy 4:8

5Therefore judge nothing before the time, until the Lord comes, who will both bring to light the hidden things of darkness and reveal the counsels of the hearts. Then each one's praise will come from God.   —1 Corinthians 4:5

18The nations were angry, and Your wrath has come, and the time of the dead, that they should be judged, and that You should reward Your servants the prophets and the saints, and those who fear Your name, small and great, and should destroy those who destroy the earth.
                    —Revelation 11:18

This last Scripture is a part of the seventh or last trumpet, at which time the saints are caught up into the air to be with Jesus. The order of events will be: 1) the rapture, when corruption and mortality put on incorruption and immortality; 2) a rendezvous in the air with Jesus; 3) the Behma where we are examined and compensated with rewards for our faithfulness.

Who will judge the believers? Jesus is declared to be the righteous judge.

22For the Father judges no one, but has committed all judgment to the Son, 23that all should honor the Son just as they honor the Father.   —John 5:22-23

For the believer, the end game of the Behma is to one day hear Jesus speak the words, "Well done, good and faithful servant; you were faithful over a few things, I will make you ruler over many things. Enter into the joy of your lord" (Matthew 25:21).

The Marriage and the Marriage Supper

Often scholars treat the marriage of the Lamb and the marriage supper of the Lamb as being one and the same. They are two distinct events, even as today's wedding and wedding reception are two distinct events.

To really understand the significance of these two biblical events, we need to view them as the customs of ancient Israel. To view these events from modern-day wedding customs of the West would cause us to misunderstand significant details of these end time prophetic events. Typically, today, the steps of marriage begin with dating, followed by engagement, followed by the wedding and finally the wedding reception or celebration. Jewish tradition was quite different. Often marriages were pre-arranged by both sets of parents well before the son and daughter were of age. When the two were of age, the process officially began with betrothal, in which a legally binding contract was signed by both parties. This step between Christ and His bride is already done. It happened when He came to this earth, which is the home of His bride-to-be.

> [2]For I am jealous over you with godly jealousy: for I have espoused you to one husband, that I may present you as a chaste virgin to Christ.   —2 Corinthians 11:2 KJV

After the betrothal, the Bridegroom returned with His Father to His Father's house to prepare a place for them to live. This place was built at the Father's residence. This phase was accomplished when Jesus ascended back to His Father's home in heaven.

> [2]In my Father's house are many mansions: if it were not so, I would have told you. I go to prepare a place for you. [3]And if I go and prepare a place for you, I will come again, and receive you unto myself; that where I am, there ye may be also.   —John 14:2-3 KJV

When the father of the bridegroom was satisfied that all preparations were completed by his son to begin his new family, the father released him to go fetch his bride-to-be. He and his wedding party began their procession to the house of the bride. As he drew near to her father's house, a shofar (trumpet) was blown to signal the bride and her party of his arrival. She and her party then went out to meet her bridegroom at a point between her father's house and his father's house. So it will be when Jesus comes for His bride. As He comes near where she dwells, He signals His coming with a sound of a shofar or trumpet. I believe this will happen at the last or seventh trumpet, at which sounding the bride will go out to meet her Bridegroom in the air.

According to the custom, after the bride went out to meet the groom, he proceeded back to his father's house to present his espoused bride to his father. Then the bride and the groom entered into the place prepared earlier by the bridegroom to consummate the marriage. Upon the announcement that the marriage had been consummated, the marriage supper or wedding feast began to be celebrated.

John's vision in the book of Revelation pictures the wedding feast or marriage supper of the Lamb after the marriage had already been consummated. The implication is that the coming for His bride (the rapture), the judgment seat of Christ, and the marriage had already taken place. All of this takes place before the second coming of Christ with His saints to the earth.

Concerning the identity of the bridegroom, there is no doubt. He is the Son of the Heavenly Father. He is the Son of the King in the parable of Matthew 22. This can be none other than Jesus Christ. He identifies Himself as the Bridegroom spoken of in the parable of the ten virgins in Matthew 25:10-13.

However, concerning the identity of the bride, there are some differences of opinions. Some say the bride is Israel. Others say the bride is the church. Yet others say the bride is all believers of all ages. Let us take a closer look at each of these in their listed order.

First, let us consider Israel. I don't believe this opinion is correct, because Israel has already been married. When speaking of Israel it is said, "Thy Maker is thine husband" (Isaiah 54:5-8). Even though God has divorced her for her adulteries, He has promised that the day will come when He will take her back to be His wife. She will not be taken back as a virgin, but as a wife. The Scriptures clearly declare the Lamb's bride will be a virgin in the day this wedding transpires. It is a virgin that the Lamb (Christ) is to marry. So the wife (Israel) of the Old Testament cannot be the bride of the New Testament. Also, God's restored wife is to reside in the earthly Jerusalem in earthly bodies during the millennium, while the virgin bride will preside with Christ over the entire earth in glorified bodies as the heavenly Jerusalem. On this basis, it would hard to view Israel as the "bride" of Christ.

Now let us consider the church. In identifying the virgin that Paul speaks of betrothing to Christ in 2 Corinthians 11:2, we must look to whom this epistle was written. Second Corinthians 1:1 leaves no doubt as to whom Paul was addressing in this letter.

[1]Paul, an apostle of Jesus Christ by the will of God, and Timothy our brother, to the church of God which is at Corinth, with all the saints who are in all Achaia.

—2 Corinthians 1:1

Also, in his epistle to the church at Ephesus, Paul compares the relationship that husbands and wives have with each other as being like unto that which Christ has with His church.

[22]Wives, submit to your own husbands, as to the Lord. [23]For the husband is head of the wife, as also Christ is head of the church; and He is the Savior of the body. [24]Therefore, just as the church is subject to Christ, so let the wives be to their own husbands in everything. [25]Husbands, love your wives, just as Christ also loved the church and gave Himself for her, [26]that He might sanctify and cleanse her with the washing of water by the word, [27]that He might present her to Himself a glorious church, not having spot or wrinkle or any such thing, but that she should be holy and without blemish. [28]So husbands ought to love their own wives as their own bodies; he who loves his wife loves himself. [29]For no one ever hated his own flesh, but nourishes and cherishes it, just as the Lord does the church. [30]For we are members of His body, of His flesh and of His bones. [31]"For this reason a man shall leave his father and mother and be joined to his wife, and the two shall become one flesh." [32]This is a great mystery, but I speak concerning Christ and the church.

—Ephesians 5:22-32

From this passage we learn that man is to be head of the wife like Christ is of the church. We see Christ identifying the church as the wife He gives Himself for, sanctifies and cleanses, in order that He might present her to Himself as a glorious church (wife).

He identifies her as being members of His body, of His flesh, and
of His bones. And finally, in Ephesians 5:31-32, He describes
the joining of a husband and wife in marriage (the two becoming one flesh) as a shadow picture of that mysterious relationship
that Christ has with the church (His wife). We must not forget
that there are "two brides" mentioned in the Scriptures – one in
the Old Testament and the other in the New. The one in the Old
Testament is Israel, God's bride. The one in the New Testament is
the church, the bride of Christ. The book of Revelation describes
the Lamb's wife as a holy city prepared as a bride adorned for her
husband. This Scripture portrays the bride of Christ as the "New
Jerusalem."

> ²Then I, John, saw the holy city, New Jerusalem, com-
> ing down out of heaven from God, prepared as a bride
> adorned for her husband. ⁹Then one of the seven angels
> who had the seven bowls filled with the seven last plagues
> came to me and talked with me, saying, "Come, I will
> show you the bride, the Lamb's wife." ¹⁰And he carried
> me away in the Spirit to a great and high mountain, and
> showed me the great city, the holy Jerusalem, descending
> out of heaven from God.   —Revelation 21:2, 9-10

Is this "city" figurative speech for the bride of Christ? This
shouldn't be too hard to imagine. When you consider the two
women we discussed in detail in chapter 26 of this book being lik-
ened unto cities, it is easy to see the New Jerusalem as being the
bride of Christ (Revelation 3:12; 21:2; 11:1-2; even as the other
woman, the harlot, is referred to as a city in Revelation 14:8; 17:18).

Finally, let us consider the possibility of the bride consisting of all
believers of all ages. If that were true, there would be no earthly representation at the wedding except the bride. I believe the Scriptures

teach that there will be others from the earth invited to the wedding in addition to the bride. In describing the body of Christ in 1 Corinthians 12, Paul writes that the body has many parts. If the whole body were only one or two parts, where would the body be?

> [17]If the whole body were an eye, where would be the hearing? If the whole were hearing, where would be the smelling? [18]But now God has set the members, each one of them, in the body just as He pleased. [19]And if they were all one member, where would the body be? [20]But now indeed there are many members, yet one body.
> —1 Corinthians 12:17-20

Everyone knows weddings are not only attended by the bride and the groom but also invited guests. It is no different with the wedding of Christ and His bride. Attending the wedding feast will be not only the church as the bride of Christ, but others as well. In attendance will be family and friends of the bride and the groom. There will be heavenly guests and earthly guests. I believe the other earthly guests would include the Old Testament saints before and after the flood. Another possibility might be those who are saved during the great tribulation through the ministry of the sun-clad woman (the church). John the Baptist, one of the last Old Testament saints, identified himself as being a friend of the Bridegroom in John 3:29. The angel in Revelation told John to write, "Blessed are those who are invited to the marriage supper of the Lamb" (Revelation 19:9). The marriage supper of the Lamb is a glorious celebration of all who are in Christ! However, I do not believe all earthly attendees will be a part of the bride of Christ.

> [9]Then he said to me, "Write: 'Blessed are those who are called to the marriage supper of the Lamb!'" And he said

to me, "These are the true sayings of God."
—**Revelation 19:9**

According to this passage, wedding guests will be called to the marriage supper of the Lamb, not the wedding, and those who are called will be blessed. My conclusion therefore is that since wedding guests are not the bride, the guests at the marriage supper of the Lamb will not be part of Christ's bride, the church. However since the guests at the marriage supper of the Lamb will be blessed and will be in heaven, they must all be believers who are a part of the first resurrection (Revelation 20:6). The fact that all guests will be believers but not part of the church leads to the presumption that not all believers of all ages are members of the church. This is not to imply that the Old Testament saints are inferior to the church, but merely to point out the blessedness of the privilege of being part of the church. I personally believe that the Old Testament saints of Israel will be restored forever as the wife of the living God during the millennial kingdom and into the eternal state.

Before concluding this topic, I would like to address the proper wedding attire of the bride and those invited to the marriage supper (feast) of the Lamb. First let's look at the bride's attire. Weddings require a lot of planning. For the bride, much of that planning has to do with her attire. She gives much attention to finding a dress that brings out her beauty, then the matching shoes and the appropriate jewelry. Jeremiah 2:32 (KJV) says, "Can a maid forget her ornaments, or a bride her attire?" Obviously that is meant to be a rhetorical question. Would it then seem likely that even greater significance would be placed on these things in preparation for the greatest wedding of all time? John describes the attire of Jesus' bride in Revelation chapter 19:

7"Let us be glad and rejoice and give Him glory, for the marriage of the Lamb has come, and His wife has made herself ready." 8And to her it was granted to be arrayed in fine linen, clean and bright, for the fine linen is the righteous acts of the saints.   —Revelation 19:7-8

Her gown is made of fine linen, clean and bright, which is the righteous acts of the saints. Notice it explicitly says that Jesus' wife has made herself ready, which would indicate that the righteous acts were her doing. This righteousness is not a result of the imputed righteousness of the finished works of Jesus Christ but rather the result of her own works done prior to the wedding while in her earthly home. These works did not earn her place as the heavenly bride, but they did affect the quality of the attire she would wear at the wedding. Only the righteous acts of Jesus imputed to our account determine our heavenly destination. However, the quality of life in that destination has very much to do with the works we do while in our natural bodies. This does not infer that all the works she did while on the earth were perfect or righteous. However, once she goes out to meet her bridegroom, there is the judgment seat of Christ where all her works will be tried by fire. Any works found lacking will be burned up until all that would defile is consumed and she is left spotless. It is important to remember that when she goes out to meet her bridegroom she does not have her wedding attire on. The bride does not adorn herself until just prior to her wedding.

Not only does the bride need to be properly attired for the wedding but so do the guests. There is a dress code for all invited guests who will be attending the wedding. All that would be improper or defiled attire must be removed and replaced with adornment befitting the occasion and place. Like the bride, so will all the guests pass through the judgment seat of Christ, that all that is not befitting is removed. If not properly attired, they were not permitted into the marriage supper. The parable in Matthew 22:11-14 makes this point; the king saw one of the guests without a wedding garment on and asked him to leave. Remember, this was a royal wedding and the attire must be fitting of royalty. Revelation chapter 4 gives us a glimpse of what proper royal attire might look like in heaven.

> [4]Around the throne were twenty-four thrones, and on the thrones I saw twenty-four elders sitting, clothed in white robes; and they had crowns of gold on their heads.
> —Revelation 4:4

I personally believe the description of the twenty-four elders sitting on their thrones with golden crowns on their heads is parabolic language representative of the Old Testament believers and the New Testament church. In the end, all who have crowns upon their heads will gladly cast them at the feet of Jesus to show honor to Him, without whom there would be no good works.

After all of these festivities, Jesus will begin to prepare His saints to be part of that great, heavenly army that will do battle with Him against His earthly enemies.

28

The Rapture and After
(part 2)

The Second Coming

What happens after the marriage supper? Usually a bridegroom and the bride exchange their wedding garments for traveling attire so that they might go off to spend some alone time together. Generally, this is to some pleasure resort or place that they may have never seen. Often it is a trip to some distant land. Sometimes it is a visit to the old home of the bride, to spend time there. So it will be after the marriage supper of the Lamb. The heavenly Bridegroom will take His bride on a trip, and to what more suitable place can they go than back to the old home of the bride (the earth) to spend time together where she used to live – the place where He and His lordship had been rejected earlier. This time the whole earth will know that He was and is the King of kings and Lord of lords. They will know that He is truly the Son of God and that His wife, the church, is His chosen bride (His queen) who will rule and reign with Him over the whole earth.

This coming to the earth with His saints after the marriage feast is referred to theologically as the second coming of Christ. At this coming, He will descend out of heaven on a white horse, followed by His armies on their white horses.

> [11]Now I saw heaven opened, and behold, a white horse. And He who sat on him was called Faithful and True, and in righteousness He judges and makes war. [12]His eyes were like a flame of fire, and on His head were many crowns. He had a name written that no one knew except Himself. [13]He was clothed with a robe dipped in blood, and His name is called The Word of God. [14]And the armies in heaven, clothed in fine linen, white and clean, followed Him on white horses. [15]Now out of His mouth goes a sharp sword, that with it He should strike the nations. And He Himself will rule them with a rod of iron. He Himself treads the winepress of the fierceness and wrath of Almighty God. [16]And He has on His robe and on His thigh a name written: KING OF KINGS AND LORD OF LORDS.   —Revelation 19:11-16

He and His armies will touch down on the Mount of Olives where all the armies of all the nations of this world will have gathered to destroy Israel and the holy city of Jerusalem. Throughout the ages the devil has put into the hearts of men an obsession to exterminate Israel, the chosen nation of God, and to control and inhabit the city of Jerusalem. Even today we are hearing the rhetoric of numerous nations with this obsession going unchallenged by the nations of this world. Where is the outrage? Would the nations who are silent find this rhetoric acceptable if they were the targets of such hatred? I don't think so! However, the second coming will be a day of the vengeance of our God upon all the nations for atrocities committed against God's chosen people. It will mark the culmination of 3½ years of judgment referred to as "the great day of God's wrath." This coming is a part of the judgment of the seventh trumpet/bowl. At the time of His earthly touchdown, the nations will have overrun half of Jerusalem and killed two-thirds of the Jewish inhabitants. When Jesus' feet touch the mount, a great earthquake will occur which will cause the mountain to cleave in two. The valley created by this earthquake will provide a way for the remaining Israelis to escape the city and meet with and see the one whom they have pierced on the cross. They will recognize that the promised Messiah is the very Jesus they had rejected. They will become believers and, in fact, will be the only believers here on earth that are yet in natural bodies. These will join with the Lord and His armies to fight and prevail against the armies of this world in that great battle called Armageddon. The Lord will use this battle, as well as the other previous judgments, to deliver the earth of its most vile influences. The earth will be ridded of the most wicked of men during the time of God's great wrath. At the conclusion of the battle of Armageddon, the Lord will capture the beast and the false prophet and cast them alive into the lake of fire so they no longer can negatively influence and deceive the inhabitants of this earth.

> [19]And I saw the beast, the kings of the earth, and their armies, gathered together to make war against Him who sat on the horse and against His army. [20]Then the beast was captured, and with him the false prophet who worked signs in his presence, by which he deceived those who received the mark of the beast and those who worshiped his image. These two were cast alive into the lake of fire burning with brimstone. [21]And the rest were killed

with the sword which proceeded from the mouth of Him who sat on the horse. And all the birds were filled with their flesh.   —Revelation 19:19-21

The devil, however, will be taken, chained, and cast into the bottomless pit for a thousand years, that he would not be able to deceive the nations any more until the end of the thousand years.

> ¹Then I saw an angel coming down from heaven, having the key to the bottomless pit and a great chain in his hand. ²He laid hold of the dragon, that serpent of old, who is the Devil and Satan, and bound him for a thousand years; ³and he cast him into the bottomless pit, and shut him up, and set a seal on him, so that he should deceive the nations no more till the thousand years were finished. But after these things he must be released for a little while.   —Revelation 20:1-3

We, the saints, will be here to rule and reign with Christ in our glorified bodies for a thousand years. The elect remnant of Israel that is now saved will be established as a kingdom of priests to this earth. They will accept the very priesthood they rejected earlier through the ministry of Moses. They, as priests who have access to God, will exercise their priesthood to those earthlings who do not have access to God. Through their priesthood, salvation will come to many who dwell on the earth.

> ⁴And I saw thrones, and they sat on them, and judgment was committed to them. Then I saw the souls of those who had been beheaded for their witness to Jesus and for the word of God, who had not worshiped the beast or his image, and had not received his mark on their foreheads or on their hands. And they lived and reigned with Christ for a thousand years.   —Revelation 20:4

The Millennial Kingdom

The millennial kingdom re-establishes the edenic state (the Garden of Eden) where once again peace, prosperity, health, longevity, joy, rejoicing, holiness, and absence of the curses (i.e., thorns, thistles, weeds, pestilences, poisonous snakes, etc.) are all established on the earth (Micah 4:1-5; Isaiah 11:5-10; 32:13-18; Zechariah 14:8-11). Eden was a mix of both natural and supernatural trees. It was God's kingdom on this earth which man was to export to the four corners of the earth. When man sinned, he was banished from the garden (or kingdom of God) on the earth.

In the beginning, God gave the dominion over this earth to man. Man abdicated this charge and Satan usurped man's God-given role. For six millenniums, God has tolerated the mismanagement of this earth by man and Satan. God's purposed plan from the beginning will finally find its fulfillment during the seventh millennium. Christ will establish His rule and reign on the earth for one thousand years. He once again will give to man that portion of God's authority which is the earth.

> [16]The heaven, even the heavens, are the Lord's; but the earth He has given to the children of men.
> —Psalms 115:16

> [4]And I saw thrones, and they sat on them, and judgment was committed to them. Then I saw the souls of those who had been beheaded for their witness to Jesus and for the word of God, who had not worshiped the beast or his image, and had not received his mark on their foreheads or on their hands. And they lived and reigned with Christ for a thousand years. [5]But the rest of the dead did not live again until the thousand years were finished. This is the

first resurrection. ⁶Blessed and holy is he who has part in the first resurrection. Over such the second death has no power, but they shall be priests of God and of Christ, and shall reign with Him a thousand years.

—Revelation 20:4-6

Christ's bride (the church) shall reign with Him for a thousand years. What about Israel? The prophet Isaiah, in speaking of the millennial kingdom, says that God will take Israel back as His wife. He will bless her who was once forsaken for her adulteries and establish her righteousness. The Gentiles will see her righteousness and the brightness of her glory and will declare her state of blessedness.

> ¹⁰I will greatly rejoice in the Lord, My soul shall be joyful in my God; for He has clothed me with the garments of salvation, He has covered me with the robe of righteousness, as a bridegroom decks himself with ornaments, and as a bride adorns herself with her jewels. —Isaiah 61:10

> ¹For Zion's sake I will not hold My peace, and for Jerusalem's sake I will not rest, until her righteousness goes forth as brightness, and her salvation as a lamp that burns. ²The Gentiles shall see your righteousness, and all kings your glory. You shall be called by a new name, which the mouth of the Lord will name. ³You shall also be a crown of glory in the hand of the Lord, and a royal diadem in the hand of your God. ⁴You shall no longer be termed Forsaken, nor shall your land any more be termed Desolate; but you shall be called Hephzibah, and your land Beulah; for the Lord delights in you, and your land shall be married. ⁵For as a young man marries a virgin, so shall your sons marry you; and as the bridegroom rejoices over the bride, so shall your God rejoice over you.

> —Isaiah 62:1-5

When God does this, He will declare that she shall no longer be termed or named "forsaken" but shall be called *Hephzibah*. This word in the Hebrew means, "My delight is in her"; it also refers to a queen of a king. God goes on to say that Israel will be called "married" instead of forsaken or divorced.

At the end of the millennium, He will loose the devil out of the bottomless pit for a short season to once again deceive, tempt, and influence those who are not the true worshippers of God.

> **[7]Now when the thousand years have expired, Satan will be released from his prison [8]and will go out to deceive the nations which are in the four corners of the earth, Gog and Magog, to gather them together to battle, whose number is as the sand of the sea. [9]They went up on the breadth of the earth and surrounded the camp of the saints and the beloved city. And fire came down from God out of heaven and devoured them. [10]The devil, who deceived them, was cast into the lake of fire and brimstone where the beast and the false prophet are. And they will be tormented day and night forever and ever.**
>
> **—Revelation 20:7-10**

As we have said earlier, true worshippers are those who worship God in spirit and truth in the inward parts of their being. Even during the millennial kingdom, without the influence of the devil and his workers, there will continue to exist the "tale of the two women" as discussed earlier in chapter 26 of this book. Co-existing together on this earth, the two women will outwardly serve the Lord God. However, those who only worship God externally will be influenced and led astray by the devil at the end of the age. They will unite with him, pledge allegiance to him, and will enlist in the devil's army in an attempt to overthrow the nation of Israel.

This will culminate in that great and final battle called Gog and Magog in which the devil and his massive army will surround and fight against the saints of God and the city of Jerusalem. God will utterly destroy His opposers by sending down fire from heaven. He will cast the devil into the lake of fire where the beast and false prophet are to be tormented day and night forever and ever.

The Great White Throne Judgment

Immediately following the battle of Gog and Magog, God will appear on a great white throne to bring His final judgment on this earth and its inhabitants, whether they be spirit beings or human beings. All of mankind that was not a part of the judgment at the Behma seat will stand before God to be judged at the end of the millennium. They will be judged for the works they did while in their mortal bodies. Just as there are degrees of rewards for the saints for their works, so shall there also be degrees of everlasting punishment for unbelievers for their works.

> [13]"Woe to you, Chorazin! Woe to you, Bethsaida! For if the mighty works which were done in you had been done in Tyre and Sidon, they would have repented long ago, sitting in sackcloth and ashes. [14]But it will be more tolerable for Tyre and Sidon at the judgment than for you.
> —Luke 10:13-14

It seems people will have to answer for all the opportunities God gave them throughout their lives to receive His grace – the greater the opportunity, the greater the accountability. Jesus taught that to whom much is given, much is required. This part of the judgment has nothing to do with a person's eternal destination. It simply determines the quality of either destination.

> [11]Then I saw a great white throne and Him who sat on it, from whose face the earth and the heaven fled away. And there was found no place for them. [12]And I saw the dead, small and great, standing before God, and books were opened. And another book was opened, which is the Book of Life. And the dead were judged according to their works, by the things which were written in the books. [13]The sea gave up the dead who were in it, and Death and Hades delivered up the dead who were in them. And they were judged, each one according to his works. [14]Then Death and Hades were cast into the lake of fire. This is the second death. [15]And anyone not found written in the Book of Life was cast into the lake of fire.
> —Revelation 20:11-15

It is interesting to note that hell and the grave will deliver up all the dead within her, and all (100%) will be cast into the lake of fire, which is the second death. Concerning those who are alive when this judgment takes place, they too will be judged. Some will go to the left as goats and some to the right as sheep. Whoever is not found written in the Lamb's Book of Life will be cast into the lake of fire. Those whose names are written in the Book will enter into the joy of God's rest to forever be with the Lord God. This begins the eternal state.

The Eternal State

In the eternal state, God will bring many changes to what mankind has ever known on this earth. One such change is that time will be no more. It will be about a present state of being. Some will inherit eternal life, which is a never-ending present tense union with the Great "I AM," where the past and future no longer exist. Unbelievers will inherit eternal death, which is a never-ending present tense separation from the presence of God. These will not be consumed in the fire and cease to exist as some teach. Jesus describes this judgment as everlasting punishment in Matthew 25:

> [46]And these will go away into everlasting punishment, but the righteous into eternal life."
> —Matthew 25:46

Another major change will be a doing away with the old and the bringing in of the new. The old heavens and earth will pass away and God will make a new heaven and a new earth.

> [1]Now I saw a new heaven and a new earth, for the first heaven and the first earth had passed away. Also there was no more sea. [2]Then I, John, saw the holy city, New Jerusalem, coming down out of heaven from God, prepared as a bride adorned for her husband. [3]And I heard a loud voice from heaven saying, "Behold, the tabernacle of God is with men, and He will dwell with them, and they shall be His people. God Himself will be with them and be their God. [4]And God will wipe away every tear from their eyes; there shall be no more death, nor sorrow, nor crying. There shall be no more pain, for the former things have passed away." [5]Then He who sat on the throne said, "Behold, I make all things new." And He said to me, "Write, for these words are true and faithful.
> —Revelation 21:1-5

Notice that the new earth will have no seas. Imagine the entire globe without any oceans or seas. There will be no sun or moon to light it. The glory of God will illuminate the new earth. There will be no night any longer, because this glory will always be.

²²But I saw no temple in it, for the Lord God Almighty and the Lamb are its temple. ²³The city had no need of the sun or of the moon to shine in it, for the glory of God illuminated it. The Lamb is its light. ²⁴And the nations of those who are saved shall walk in its light, and the kings of the earth bring their glory and honor into it. ²⁵Its gates shall not be shut at all by day (there shall be no night there). ²⁶And they shall bring the glory and the honor of the nations into it. ²⁷But there shall by no means enter it anything that defiles, or causes an abomination or a lie, but only those who are written in the Lamb's Book of Life.   —Revelation 21:22-27

There will be no more tears, death, sorrow, crying, nor pain. All these former things will pass away and be replaced with the loving, glorious presence of the Living God forever.

³And I heard a loud voice from heaven saying, "Behold, the tabernacle of God is with men, and He will dwell with them, and they shall be His people. God Himself will be with them and be their God. ⁴And God will wipe away every tear from their eyes; there shall be no more death, nor sorrow, nor crying. There shall be no more pain, for the former things have passed away.   —Revelation 21:3-4

The testimony of this last book of the Bible ends with a loving invitation to "come" to experience that which God has prepared for those who love Him.

Epilogue

In writing this book, it was my goal to keep its length to approximately two hundred pages. Originally it was my plan to have three sections. Section One speaks to what Jesus taught about eschatology while He was on the earth. Section Two speaks to what Jesus taught about eschatology from heaven through His apostles and prophets. Section Three was to be entitled, "From Now to Eternity," which was to establish a chronological timeline of events that must yet happen. However, as Sections One and Two became about 300 pages, I felt the Lord would have me cover Section Three in a future book as a sequel.

In the sequel, I plan to relate in greater detail the prophecies of Daniel with those of the book of Revelation. I want to take an in-depth look at the 70 weeks of Daniel in relationship to the 2,000 year church age interval. I want to deal with the question, "Is there to be a 2,000 year gap between the 69th and 70th weeks of Daniel?"

Other events and topics to be discussed in the sequel would include the battle of Gog and Magog, the four severe judgments of Ezekiel, the fulfillment of the fall feasts by Jesus, the various time periods prophesied in Daniel chapter 12, and the building of a timeline of the events and topics discussed.

Appendix A

Day of the Lord Scriptures

(translations are either NKJV or KJV)

¹²And I beheld when he had opened the sixth seal, and, lo, there was a great earthquake; and the sun became black as sackcloth of hair, and the moon became as blood;   —Revelation 6:12

¹³And the stars of heaven fell unto the earth, even as a fig tree casteth her untimely figs, when she is shaken of a mighty wind.
          —Revelation 6:13

¹⁴And the heaven departed as a scroll when it is rolled together; and every mountain and island were moved out of their places.
          —Revelation 6:14

¹⁵And the kings of the earth, and the great men, and the rich men, and the chief captains, and the mighty men, and every bondman, and every free man, hid themselves in the dens and in the rocks of the mountains;   —Revelation 6:15

¹⁶And said to the mountains and rocks, fall on us, and hide us from the face of him that sits on the throne, and from the wrath of the Lamb: —Revelation 6:16

[17]For the great day of his wrath is come; and who shall be able to stand?   —Revelation 6:17

[1]Blow ye the trumpet in Zion, and sound an alarm in my holy mountain: let all the inhabitants of the land tremble: for the day of the Lord cometh, for it is nigh at hand;   —Joel 2:1

[2]A day of darkness and of gloominess, a day of clouds and of thick darkness, as the morning spread upon the mountains: a great people and a strong; there hath not been ever the like, neither shall be any more after it, even to the years of many generations.   —Joel 2:2

[30]And I will show wonders in the heavens and in the earth, blood, and fire, and pillars of smoke.   —Joel 2:30

[31]The sun shall be turned into darkness, and the moon into blood, before the great and the terrible day of the Lord come.   —Joel 2:31

[15]The sun and the moon shall be darkened, and the stars shall withdraw their shining.   —Joel 3:15

[29]Immediately after the tribulation of those days shall the sun be darkened, and the moon shall not give her light, and the stars shall fall from heaven, and the powers of the heavens shall be shaken: —Matthew 24:29

[30]Then the sign of the Son of Man will appear in heaven, and then all the tribes of the earth will mourn, and they will see the Son of Man coming on the clouds of heaven with power and great glory.   —Matthew 24:30

[24]But in those days, after that tribulation, the sun shall be darkened, and the moon shall not give her light...   —Mark 13:24

[25]And the stars of heaven shall fall, and the powers that are in heaven shall be shaken.   —Mark 13:25

[25]And there shall be signs in the sun, and in the moon, and in the stars; and upon the earth distress of nations, with perplexity; the sea and the waves roaring;   —Luke 21:25

[26]Men's hearts failing them from fear and the expectation of those things which are coming on the earth, for the powers of the heavens will be shaken.   —Luke 21:26

[27]Then they will see the Son of Man coming in a cloud with power and great glory.   —Luke 21:27

[6]Howl ye; for the day of the Lord is at hand; it shall come as a destruction from the Almighty.   —Isaiah 13:6

[7]Therefore shall all hands be faint, and every man's heart shall melt: —Isaiah 13:7

[8]And they shall be afraid: pangs and sorrows shall take hold of them; they shall be in pain as a woman that travails: they shall be amazed one at another; their faces shall be as flames.
                              —Isaiah 13:8

[9]Behold, the day of the Lord cometh, cruel both with wrath and fierce anger, to lay the land desolate: and he shall destroy the sinners thereof out of it.   —Isaiah 13:9

[10]For the stars of heaven and the constellations thereof shall not give their light: the sun shall be darkened in his going forth, and the moon shall not cause her light to shine.   —Isaiah 13:10

[11]And I will punish the world for their evil, and the wicked for their iniquity; and I will cause the arrogance of the proud to cease, and will lay low the haughtiness of the terrible.
                                                        —Isaiah 13:11

[7]And when I shall put thee out, I will cover the heaven, and make the stars thereof dark; I will cover the sun with a cloud, and the moon shall not give her light.   —Ezekiel 32:7

[8]All the bright lights of heaven will I make dark over thee, and set darkness upon thy land, saith the Lord God.
                                                        —Ezekiel 32:8

[17]And it shall come to pass in the last days, saith God, I will pour out of my Spirit upon all flesh: and your sons and your daughters shall prophesy, and your young men shall see visions, and your old men shall dream dreams: —Acts 2:17

[18]And on my servants and on my handmaidens I will pour out in those days of my Spirit; and they shall prophesy: —Acts 2:18

[19]And I will show wonders in heaven above, and signs in the earth beneath; blood, and fire, and vapour of smoke:
                                                        —Acts 2:19

[20]The sun shall be turned into darkness, and the moon into blood, before the great and notable day of the Lord come:
                                                        —Acts 2:20

[14]The great day of the Lord is near, it is near, and hastens greatly, even the voice of the day of the Lord: the mighty man shall cry there bitterly.   —Zephaniah 1:14

[15]That day is a day of wrath, a day of trouble and distress, a day of wastedness and desolation, a day of darkness and gloominess, a day of clouds and thick darkness,   —Zephaniah 1:15

[16]A day of the trumpet and alarm against the fenced cities, and against the high towers.   —Zephaniah 1:16

[17]And I will bring distress upon men, that they shall walk like blind men, because they have sinned against the Lord: and their blood shall be poured out as dust, and their flesh as the dung.
                                                    —Zephaniah 1:17

[18]Neither their silver nor their gold shall be able to deliver them in the day of the Lord's wrath; but the whole land shall be devoured by the fire of his jealousy: for he shall make even a speedy riddance of all them that dwell in the land.   —Zephaniah 1:18

[29]For, behold, the days are coming, in the which they shall say, Blessed are the barren, and the wombs that never bare, and the paps which never gave suck.   —Luke 23:29

[30]Then shall they begin to say to the mountains, Fall on us; and to the hills, Cover us.   —Luke 23:30

[1]For, behold, the day cometh, that shall burn as an oven; and all the proud, yea, and all that do wickedly, shall be stubble: and the day that cometh shall burn them up, saith the Lord of hosts, that it shall leave them neither root nor branch.   —Malachi 4:1

²But who may abide the day of his coming? and who shall stand when he appears? for he is like a refiner's fire, and like fullers' soap: —Malachi 3:2

¹¹The lofty looks of man shall be humbled, and the haughtiness of men shall be bowed down, and the Lord alone shall be exalted in that day.   —Isaiah 2:11

¹²For the day of the Lord of hosts shall be upon every one that is proud and lofty, and upon every one that is lifted up; and he shall be brought low: —Isaiah 2:12

¹³And upon all the cedars of Lebanon, that are high and lifted up, and upon all the oaks of Bashan,   —Isaiah 2:13

¹⁴And upon all the high mountains, and upon all the hills that are lifted up,   —Isaiah 2:14

¹⁵And upon every high tower, and upon every fenced wall,   —Isaiah 2:15

¹⁶And upon all the ships of Tarshish, and upon all pleasant pictures.   —Isaiah 2:16

¹⁷And the loftiness of man shall be bowed down, and the haughtiness of men shall be made low: and the Lord alone shall be exalted in that day.   —Isaiah 2:17

²⁵Not forsaking the assembling of ourselves together, as the manner of some is; but exhorting one another: and so much the more, as ye see the day approaching.   —Hebrew 10:25

Appendix B

Trumpets & Bowls Comparison

TRUMPET 1 ~ REV. 8:7 Affects the earth, trees, & green grass	**BOWL 1 ~ REV. 16:1-2** Affects the earth
TRUMPET 2 ~ REV. 8:8-9 Affects the sea, living creatures in the sea, & the ships	**BOWL 2 ~ REV. 16:3** Affects the sea & living creatures in the sea
TRUMPET 3 ~ REV. 8:10-11 Affects rivers & fountains of water (fresh water supplies)	**BOWL 3 ~ REV. 16:4-7** Affects rivers & fountains of water (fresh water supplies)
TRUMPET 4 ~ REV. 8:12-13 Affects the sun, moon, & stars	**BOWL 4 ~ REV. 16:8-9** Affects the sun
TRUMPET 5 ~ REV. 9:1-11 Affects the bottomless pit or the kingdom of darkness (the throne & abode of Satan & his army)	**BOWL 5 ~ REV. 16:10-11** Affects the throne of the beast or the kingdom of darkness
TRUMPET 6 ~ REV. 9:13-21 Affects the Euphrates River & prepares the way for an invasion by a vast army of 200,000,000 soldiers	**BOWL 6 ~ REV. 16:12** Affects the Euphrates River & prepares the way for an invasion by a vast army led by the kings of the east
TRUMPET 7 ~ REV. 11:15-19 Affects the kingdom of God & the kingdoms of the world Citizens of the kingdom of God (dead & alive) are caught up into the air with the Lord to be rewarded for their works Citizens of the world remain on the earth to be punished by the wrath of God for their works	**BOWL 7 ~ REV. 16:17-21** Affects the air, which is where the saints of God are caught up to meet the Lord Saints of God (dead & alive) are caught up to meet the Lord in the air —1 Thess. 4:17 Unbelievers are punished for their ungodliness by receiving the fierceness of the wrath of God

Appendix C

Olivet Discourse Signs & Seals Comparison

1st SIGN ~ MATT. 24:4-5	1st SEAL ~ REV. 6:1-2
Deception and false prophets in the world deceiving mankind	White horse with rider going forth to conquer mankind after resurrection 1 Jn. 2:18-27 (antichrist spirit already present)
2nd SIGN ~ MATT. 24:6	**2nd SEAL ~ REV. 6:3-4**
Wars and rumors of wars affect the world, not just a couple of nations WWI and WWII affected the entire world, not just a few nations Many thought this would be the end of the world but Jesus said it wouldn't be	Red horse with rider who had power to take away peace from the earth A time when men would kill each other on the earth Speaks of war affecting the whole earth
3rd SIGN ~ MATT. 24:7a	**3rd SEAL ~ REV. 6:5-6**
Nation rising against nation not in war like verse 6 but in cold war for social, economic, & military supremacy Cold war competition causes societal and economical upheavals which leads to hyper-inflation	Black horse with rider carrying balances to measure daily food supply that costs a day's wages because of inflation Delicacies like wine are very costly but still available in times of inflation; not so in times of famine (where we are currently)
4th SIGN ~ MATT. 24:7b-8	**4th SEAL ~ REV. 6:7-8**
Prophetic fulfillment of the 4 severe judgments spoken of in Ezek. 4:12-23 (famine, sword, beasts, & pestilence) These are the beginning of the birth pains that give birth to the manchild (overcomers) of Rev. 12:2-5	Pale horse with rider who brought death to many through the 4 severe judgments One fourth of the world's population will die as a result of this seal opening This is the beginning of the birth pains
5th SIGN ~ MATT. 24:9-21	**5th SEAL ~ REV. 6:9-11**
The saints are tested & purged in the great tribulation for 3½ years Many will be martyred for their faith	Souls of those martyred in the great tribulation are crying out to God No more gospel invitation to "Come"
6th SIGN ~ MATT. 24:29a	**6th SEAL ~ REV. 6:12-17**
Immediately after the tribulation, there shall be signs in the sun, moon, & stars	Immediately after the 5th seal, there shall be signs in the sun, moon, & stars
7th SIGN ~ MATT. 24:29b	**7th SEAL ~ REV. 8 & 16**
Powers/authorities in heaven & earth are judged & shaken in the GDOGW	7 trumpets/bowls of God's judgment & great wrath are released on the earth

Appendix D

Timeline

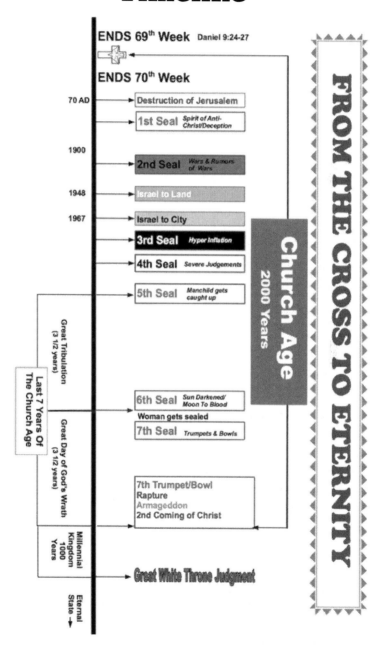

ENDS 69th Week Daniel 9:24-27

ENDS 70th Week

70 AD — Destruction of Jerusalem

1st Seal *Spirit of Anti-Christ/Deception*

1900

2nd Seal *Wars & Rumors of Wars*

1948 Israel to Land

1967 Israel to City

3rd Seal *Hyper Inflation*

4th Seal *Severe Judgements*

5th Seal *Manchild gets caught up*

Church Age
2000 Years

Great Tribulation
(3 1/2 years)

Last 7 Years Of
The Church Age

6th Seal *Sun Darkened/Moon To Blood*

Woman gets sealed

7th Seal *Trumpets & Bowls*

Great Day of God's Wrath
(3 1/2 years)

7th Trumpet/Bowl
Rapture
Armageddon
2nd Coming of Christ

Millennial
Kingdom
1000
Years

Great White Throne Judgment

Eternal
State

FROM THE CROSS TO ETERNITY

Discipleship Materials

Gary has written four levels of discipleship courses that have been used by many churches to equip members for their Christian walk and ministries. The emphasis of Discipleship 1 is "Downreach," which deals with the foundational teachings of the doctrine of Christ. The emphasis of Discipleship 2 is "Upreach," which deals with the spiritual/heavenly walk of the believer. The emphasis of Discipleship 3 is "Inreach," which deals with the interior life or internal walk of the believer. The emphasis of Discipleship 4 is "Outreach," which deals with applying the principles of the sovereignty of God to the priesthood and the ministry of the believer. Each of the above courses includes a textbook and a student workbook (available also, a teacher's edition workbook).

For more information or to order these courses, contact:

ARM Resources, www.ARMresources.org
email: arm@armresources.org

or

Apostolic Team Ministries International
www.ATMintl.org
email: atmoffice@atmintl.org (ask for ATM discount)

Made in the USA
San Bernardino, CA
05 May 2020